A HISTORY
OF THE YORKSHIRE COAST
FISHING INDUSTRY
1780-1914

Hull University Press

Occasional Papers in Regional and Local History

No. 1

A HISTORY OF THE YORKSHIRE COAST FISHING INDUSTRY 1780-1914

ROBB ROBINSON

Senior Lecturer,
Hull College of Further Education

HULL UNIVERSITY PRESS
1987

© Robb Robinson 1987

British Library Cataloguing in Publication Data

Robinson, R.
  A history of the Yorkshire coast fishing industry. —
  (Occasional papers in regional and local history; 1).
  1. Fisheries — England — Yorkshire — History
  2. Yorkshire — Industries — History
  I. Title   II. Series
  338.3′727′094281   SH258.Y67

ISBN 0-85958-468-2
ISSN 0951-8916

Phototypeset in 11 on 12pt Times and printed by the
University of Hull

Contents

Contents

Preface

This history of the Yorkshire Coast Fishing Industry originated as part of a PhD thesis of the University of Hull presented in 1985. That thesis was supervised by Mike Brown and the debts incurred for his critical encouragement can never be fully repaid.

During my research I received much help from the staff of the Brynmor Jones Library, Hull University, and their counterparts in the Local Studies Library of Hull Central Library. Much assistance was also given by the staffs of the North Yorkshire, Hull and Humberside County Record Offices while similar help was provided by the Public Record Office, Kew and Register House, Edinburgh. Thanks are also due to the South Kensington Science Museum, London and the Town Docks Museum, Hull for their permission to reproduce the illustrations in this book.

I have received ungrudging help from Dr Joyce Bellamy, Dr Tony Michell, Barbara Nield and Donald Woodward, as well as much personal encouragement from family and old friends, many of whom have supplied valuable background information. I am particularly indebted to my father, Bill Robinson, a former fisherman, as well as my late grandfather, Edmund McKee, whose reminiscences of the fish trade unwittingly planted the first seeds of this venture in my mind.

Cottingham,   Robb Robinson
Yorkshire, 1987.

List of Figures, Illustrations and Tables

Abbreviations

A. and P.	Accounts and Papers.
HCRO	Humberside County Record Office, Beverley.
KHRO	Kingston upon Hull Record Office, 79 Lowgate, Kingston upon Hull, HU1 2AA.
NEDSFCM	North Eastern District Sea Fisheries Committee Minutes, HCRO.
n.p.	No pagination.
NYCRO	North Yorkshire County Record Office.
PRO	Public Record Office, Kew.
RC	Royal Commission.
RHE	Register House, Edinburgh.
SC	Select Committee.
SCH	Scarborough Custom House.
SPL,SHCM	Scarborough Public Library, Scarborough Harbour Commissioners' Minutes.

I

The Economic and Social Background

Before overland travel was improved by turnpike roads and then railways, access to the towns and villages involved in the Yorkshire coast fishing industry was fraught with difficulty. Between the Humber and the Tees no river of any note flows into the North Sea with the exception of the Esk, which provides a fine natural harbour around which the sea port of Whitby is clustered. But the Esk was never a navigable waterway providing inland access, and travellers to and from the neighbouring coast had to contend with the formidable natural barriers of the Yorkshire Moors and Cleveland Hills. Thus Whitby acted only as an import and export centre for the Esk valley, which limited the port's trade. Even the river valley and its tributaries were not valued as lines of communication, for their gorge-like structure tended to impede the flow of traffic.[1] Before the mid-eighteenth century, moorland trackways were the sole means of travelling overland. Writing in 1779, Lionel Charlton recalled that:

> till the year 1750, all roads to Whitby lay in a state of nature, rough, rugged and uneven: it was dangerous for a man on horseback to come into the town in the winter season . . . but more so for any laden carriage to approach the place.[2]

Inaccessibility also affected the trade of the smaller communities of Staithes, Runswick and Robin Hood's Bay. Travellers visiting the coast south of Scarborough could avoid the moorland but their journey was still far from easy. The badly-drained Vale of Pickering had to be avoided at all costs and although the road from York clung to the higher ground it was in poor repair prior to

1

turnpiking. The route from Bridlington to York through Sledmere was also difficult and required the crossing of low-lying lands around the Derwent in the Vale of York. Further south it was essential to avoid the Plain of Holderness in winter for its water-logged roads were next to impassable.

In contrast to the sluggish nature of the inland trade route, traffic along the Yorkshire coast flourished and many communities looked to the sea for their prosperity. During the second half of the seventeenth century both Scarborough and Whitby acquired an enduring interest in the Newcastle to London 'sea cole' trade. Both built and owned colliers, and as their fleets grew they diversified their activities. Yorkshire coast craft became involved first in the Baltic and then in other trades. The reputation of the local shipbuilding industry can only have been enhanced by Captain James Cook's use of Whitby-built vessels on his voyages of discovery. But the importance of Scarborough and Whitby should not be allowed to overshadow the contribution of the smaller communities to this maritime prosperity. Residents of places such as Staithes, Runswick and Robin Hood's Bay invested heavily in shipping in spite of lacking full harbour facilities, while Filey people also owned vessels and Bridlington Quay possessed a small fleet. Most craft worked from London or other large ports, only returning home for repair and refitting. Shipping and shipbuilding fostered the development of ancillary trades such as ropemaking and the manufacture of sailcloth, which was produced by a combination of factory and domestic labour in and around Whitby by the early nineteenth century.

Bridlington Quay was advantageously placed for the servicing of passing merchant vessels. When north-easterly gales were blowing, fleets of passing craft might shelter for weeks in the lee of Flamborough Head waiting for favourable weather and winds, and the township's boatmen found employment ferrying food, water and other supplies to these vessels. In 1811 a spring of exceptionally pure water was discovered close to the harbour, which encouraged more passing ships to replenish their reserves while off the port.

South of Bridlington Quay the sea was more of a predator than a source of wealth. The Holderness cliffs are made of crumbly boulder clay and have been subject to an unremitting erosion by the sea, which has eaten away about three and a half miles of land

2

since Roman times. In so doing it has left previously landlocked villages perched on the cliff edge after sweeping away their more easterly neighbours. Being surrounded by rich agricultural land on three sides and open beaches devoid of any vestige of natural protection on the other, it is hardly surprising that the inhabitants of Holderness looked more to the land than the sea for their livelihoods, although the occasional looting of wrecks[3] and smuggling remained exceptions to this rule. Smuggling was of particular importance along the Yorkshire coast in the later eighteenth and early nineteenth centuries; it was considered to be socially acceptable, profits were high, and the resources of the Excise were too stretched to deter the wholesale evasion of duties. Brandy, Geneva, tobacco and tea were the main cargoes run and the Customs believed that often the whole populations of Redcar, Saltburn, Marske, Staithes, Runswick and Robin Hood's Bay were involved in the trade.[4]

One maritime pursuit closely associated with Whitby was whaling. The port's involvement with the northern whale fishery began in 1753 but was temporarily abandoned within a few years. Interest revived, as it also did in Hull, in 1766 and by 1788 the port could muster twenty whaling ships. Thereafter the fleet gradually shrank and by the early nineteenth century no more than ten craft went each year, although this was probably the most successful period in terms of catches per vessel; the field was led by Captain William Scoresby who caught no less than 249 whales, which yielded 2034 tons of oil, in ten successive voyages beginning in 1803. After 1820 Whitby's whaling industry entered a steep decline and the last whalers sailed from the port in 1837.

North of Scarborough alum processing was a significant activity from the seventeenth to the nineteenth centuries. Alum, a chemical then important in the dyeing and tanning industries, was found locally and works had been set up both inland and on the coast. Coal was shipped in by sea and when conditions were favourable vessels were beached close to the works to unload and take off the processed alum. During the nineteenth century ironstone working assumed a considerable importance. At Port Mulgrave an artificial harbour, the ruins of which can still be seen, and underground tunnels were constructed for shipping out ore. Ironworks were also built; the most successful was opened at Skinningrove in 1874 but the first, erected at Wreckhill north of Runswick Bay, had

3

only produced a few tons after its opening in 1858 when the entire site slid down the cliff and had to be abandoned.[5] Whitby's jet deposits produced a sizeable workshop industry in the nineteenth century but there were also lesser-known activities along the coast that contributed to the livelihood of the small communities: the inhabitants of Staithes found occasional employment over the summer months collecting and burning seaweed to produce kelp, used in the manufacture of alum and glass. Seabirds' eggs were also taken from the high cliffs around Flamborough Head each May and June. Boys and other persons of light weight were let down on staked ropes to collect basketfuls of eggs from the rocky ledges while being harrassed by the screaming gulls.[6]

After the turnpikes improved communications, increasing numbers of visitors arrived along the coast. In the pre-railway age a holiday was scarcely a dream for the masses. Visitors were usually wealthy and often resorted to the coast during the summer with their household entourages. But even in high summer the arrival of fashionable visitors was rarely on a scale that could disturb the traditional fabric of Yorkshire coast life. Every fishing community possessed an individuality of its own, whether in remote villages such as Runswick and Robin Hood's Bay or part of the burgeoning resorts of Scarborough and Filey. Not only did each appear to outsiders as insular and close-knit, with inhabitants intermarrying, thus perpetuating the same family fishing names for generations, but they also exhibited minor differences in custom and practice that would set them apart from their neighbours. These would be hidden from the eye of the casual observer in much the same way as the ubiquitous blue of the fishermen's 'gansey' masked the distinctive patterns knitted in each village.

Fishing and its associated activities had long occupied an important place in the economy of the Yorkshire coast. Archaeological excavations of Roman and Viking sites in York and other places have revealed that both communities were supplied with sea fish, including cod, probably from the North Sea. Monastic houses such as Fountains Abbey were provisioned with barrels of salt herrings and other fish and fishing was certainly a major source of revenue for religious institutions along the coast; the importance of fish tithes led to periodic disputes between Bridlington Priory and Whitby Abbey over who had the rights on herrings landed at Filey. In the fourteenth century continental merchants were attracted in considerable numbers during the peak herring months of August and September and they bought up large quantities which were salted and stored in barrels.[7] Richard III issued a proclamation against the participation of foreign herring fishers as it was considered to be to the detriment of the locals.[8]

In spite of its importance, the herring fishery was later to be rivalled by that for white fish. Before the early fifteenth century, Scarborough and Whitby vessels were exploiting the cod grounds off the Faroe Islands and Iceland and such activities continued into the seventeenth century.[9] However, the mid seventeenth century seems to have been a watershed for the Yorkshire coast fishing industry. The upheavals associated with the Civil War and the loss of many larger craft to the Dutch seem to have ended the northern voyages from Scarborough and Whitby.[10] Interest in the herring fishery also seems to have declined markedly, so that by the following century it was of little more than local importance. But amidst this decay there is evidence of growth. Yorkshire craft travelled in considerable numbers to Yarmouth each year to participate in its still prosperous autumn herring fishery. At other times of the year more attention was given to the white fish grounds in the North Sea, especially off the Dogger Bank where large cod were being taken.

In earlier periods a wide range of fishing vessels was to be found,[11] but from the seventeenth century onwards designs were based on variants of the age-old coble. The largest of these variants were known as five-man boats. They were already in use at Whitby before the dissolution of the monasteries to take coal to the Abbey,[12] and they are referred to in Scarborough fishermen's wills from at least the later sixteenth century. But sometime between 1650 and 1750 they evolved into single-keeled, three-masted, decked luggers which were to form the mainstay of the Yorkshire coast off-shore fleet well into the nineteenth century.

Throughout those centuries and beyond, fisherfolk had to contend with the violence of the sea and sometimes other men in their hunt for a livelihood. Their unique and often over-romanticised occupation has set them apart. Danger was ever present and death an all too constant companion. The insularity of the fishing communities and the vicissitudes and uncertainty that were part and parcel of their way of life was strongly reflected in their customs, superstitions and folklore. Naturally, these differed from neighbouring agricultural villages but even in an age when English folk tradition remained vigorous, fishing communities were considered to be strongly tinctured with superstition. Luck in particular was a commodity to be nurtured. In order, no doubt, to encourage good fortune the fishermen of sixteenth-century Redcar invited their friends to a festival held upon St Peter's Day 'with a free hearte and no show of niggardness'. Their boats were decorated, masts painted and during the course of the celebrations each craft was sprinkled with good liquor sold to the fishermen at a groat a quart.[13] At Flamborough it was considered that a good season's fishing would follow the custom of 'Raising Herrings'. When the men had left for the fishery, their wives and other folk disguised themselves, often in the garments of their male relations, and went around the village with music and laughter, visiting their neighbours' houses to receive alms and god speed.[14] Filey also maintained a tradition believed to encourage herrings. On the third Saturday night after the boats had sailed for the Yarmouth fishery, youngsters would seize all the unused wagons and carts then drag them to the cliff top, leaving them to be taken away by their owners on the Sunday morning; this ritual was believed to drive the herrings into the nets. Bad omens often deterred fishermen from sailing. If a Flamborough fisherman met a woman, a parson or a hare on his way to the boats he would turn back immediately in the belief that he would have no luck that day.[15] At Staithes it was also considered ill-luck for a fisherman to meet a woman while he walked down to the boats carrying lines on his head or nets on his shoulder. When a woman saw a fisherman approaching under such circumstances she would at once turn her back on him. All four-footed animals were also considered to be unlucky with the mention of the pig's name being the most ill-omened. Similarly, an egg was deemed so unlucky that Staithes fishermen would not call it such; they referred to it as a 'roundabout'.

As the influence of Methodism grew in the nineteenth century, many fishing families became noted for their piety, but some customs of pre-Christian origin remained. As late as the 1880s, one custom said to be secretly maintained at Staithes had ancient origins. When a fishing boat had a protracted run of bad luck the wives of the owners and crew would assemble at midnight. Then,

6

in deep silence, they would slay a pigeon whose heart was extracted, stuck full of pins and burnt over a charcoal fire. A witch was deemed the source of the bad luck although he or she was unconscious of their power of evil. While this ceremony was in progress the witch was supposed to come to the door, dragged there unwillingly by the irresistible potency of the charms and the conspirators would make the individual some propitiatory present. It was also said to be a frequent occurrence for Staithes fishermen to keep the first fish that came into the boat after many nights of catching nothing and on returning home burn it as a sacrifice to the fates.[16]

Traditional elements, therefore, still retained a strong standing in this ancient industry whose structure was the product of centuries of gradual change. Yet, for all their insularity, these somewhat remote communities were part of a complex web of regional activity that was to show itself capable of responding to and capitalising on the forces and opportunities that were to change the nature of the national economy as the Industrial Revolution gathered its early momentum. But for the late-eighteenth century fishing industry the most dramatic implications of such economic change still lay in the future.

II

The Later Eighteenth-Century Fishing Industry

By the latter part of the eighteenth century the Yorkshire coast fishing industry had assumed a form that was both complex and distinctive. Along the seaboard stretching from the Humber to the Tees more than a score of communities contained at least a few individuals who derived a livelihood from fishing (Fig. 1), and most of those involved specialised solely in this pursuit. Little evidence can be found of a dual economy, where farmers were also part-time fishermen, that was a feature of some places. The fishing communities were of differing sizes but their relative importance did not always correspond to the size of the town or village within which they were situated. There were, for example, three harbour ports — Scarborough, Whitby and Bridlington Quay — which then, as now, could claim the largest populations along the coast. The former two, and to a lesser extent the third, possessed a thriving maritime trade based largely upon the ownership, construction and servicing of merchant vessels. Yet, at that time only Scarborough ranked as an important fishing station. As late as 1817 Whitby contained just nine fishermen and three fishmongers though it had been 'a great fischar towne' in the time of Leland.[1] Most of Bridlington Quay's few cobles spent much of their time piloting or servicing passing merchant vessels,[2] and the town relied for much of its fish supply on Filey and Flamborough. Even Scarborough was of less importance as a fishing community than places such as Staithes, Robin Hood's Bay and Flamborough which specialised to a far greater degree in this activity.

Contemporary reports suggest that fishing had declined at all three harbour ports over the eighteenth century. The causes were

8

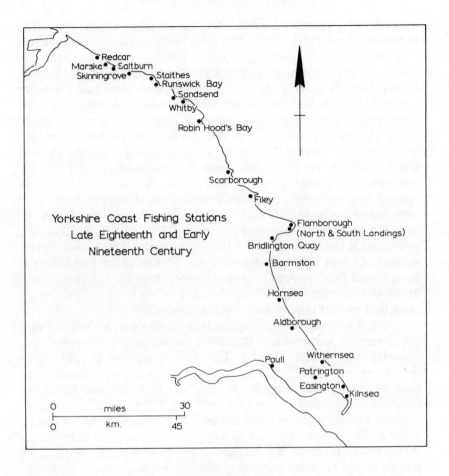

Figure 1.
Yorkshire Coast Fishing Stations Late Eighteenth Century and Early
Nineteenth Century.

Sources: Whitby, Scarborough and Bridlington Registers of Boat
Licenses; George Young, *History,* pp. 820-3.

undoubtedly associated with the vigour with which the other branches of maritime commerce were being pursued; the demands of shipbuilding, shipowning and later whaling encouraged specialisation in such areas. Communities such as Staithes, Runswick, Robin Hood's Bay, Filey and Flamborough also had extensive shipowning interests but within them fishing assumed a greater importance. These places developed the trade to an extent which more than compensated for the decline of fishing from the harbour ports. Indeed, the largest fishing station along the English coast north of the Wash was undoubtedly Staithes. In 1817, for example, the township owned a fleet of 70 cobles, each usually crewed by three men and there is no reason to suggest that there were many fewer craft in the late eighteenth century. Furthermore, over the forty years spanning the turn of the century Staithes also possessed a fleet of up to 17 five-man boats. These were three-masted, decked fishing luggers, about 53 feet in length. Between Redcar and Bridlington Quay there were about 250 small craft and up to 40 five-man boats which, because of their dimensions, were classified as first class vessels by the Customs.[3]

Along the sweep of Bridlington Bay southwards to Spurn Point the intensity with which the local communities exploited the fisheries was much lower.[4] The few boats to be found at Owthorne, Hornsea, Barmston and the like were often insufficient even to meet local demand. As late as 1848 Hornsea relied for much of its fish supply on a Flamborough fish cart which called up to three times a week in the summer.[5] The fishing tradition was so weak at Withernsea that when a small fleet was later established there it was manned by families from East Anglia. Within the mouth of the Humber important fishing stations were to be found at Patrington Haven and at Paull and they were mainly concerned with the taking of prawns and shrimps which were boiled on board the boats and then sold in towns and villages along the Humber and its tributaries.[6] Their efforts were supplemented by the occasional craft working out of other small creeks along the estuary. The shrimpers deployed a form of two netted trawl but out of season engaged in a little line fishing.

The most common activity was taking white fish by hook and line from cobles. Cobles had a long history, claimed by some to date back to Viking times, and were admirably suited to prevailing conditions, being robust and extremely seaworthy. With their double, flat-bottomed keels and sharply rising sterns they were capable of being brought ashore swiftly on relatively unsheltered beaches such as those at Redcar and Marske. There were differences of detail between cobles built at each fishing station but, whatever the variations, they were very adaptable craft used for a variety of purposes other than fishing, including pilot work and smuggling. Cobles were comparatively cheap to construct and those licensed at Bridlington Custom House between 1813 and 1820 were valued at no more than £60 new. It was rare for the owner not to be a member of the crew of three who were often related to each other, although sometimes the boat might belong to a fisherman's widow and be operated by others on her behalf. Each crew member provided a share of the fishing gear. In the case of long lining, two sets of tackle were required, for while one was being taken to sea the other was left on shore for baiting in preparation for use next day. Long lines were laid for great distances across the sea bed and attached to them were many short lines, known as snoods, with hooks on the end. For herring fishing a large number of nets was required and each crew member also provided a share of those. Whatever the fishery, income was divided amongst owners and crew on a share basis.[7]

The maximising of fishing effort each season required the existence of a well organised land-based back-up; while the crews were at sea labour had to be found to prepare the spare long lines and bait had to be collected and prepared. This again was a laborious and time-consuming task, especially when the bait, usually shell fish, was in short supply and collectors were forced to roam over greater distances in order to gather the requisite amount. Such tasks were normally carried out by the families of the crew. Herring nets were made by the older members of the community, aided by those too young for other work. Much labour was also required for the processing, storage and transportation of fish. There was thus a powerful economic incentive for fishermen to marry young and have large families which could assist with these shore-based tasks. A wife from a fishing community was an asset because she would already possess the requisite skills and be thoroughly acquainted with the demands of this rigorous way of life. This was an important reason why fishing communities tended to intermarry. In many parts of the country the fisherman's wife might be expected to carry the fish to some

11

distant market or else sell it in the surrounding villages and towns; this was the case in Northumberland and along certain stretches of the Scottish east coast. However, on the Yorkshire coast this custom, while not entirely absent, was not widespread. Most of the catch was disposed of at markets on the beach to middlemen and carried inland by trains of pannier ponies,[8] although members of fishing families might contribute to the household income through employment in these sectors.

The other main Yorkshire coast fishing activities utilised the large three-masted luggers and their range of operations made them the most important fleet of first class fishing vessels north of the Wash. As can be seen from Table 1 these vessels were owned by various fishing communities between Bridlington Quay and Staithes.

Table 1
First Class Fishing Fleets 1789 and 1825

	Staithes	Runswick	Robin Hood's Bay	Scarborough	Filey	Flamborough	Total
1789	9	6	6	4	7	4	36
1825	17	3	4	5	7	3	39

Sources: Whitby, Scarborough and Bridlington Custom House Vessel Registers.

By contemporary standards their cost was considerable, being in the region of £600, and a further £100 was required for gear and fitting out. Although called 'five-man boats', a larger crew was nearly always carried; seven were usually shipped for lining while eight or nine were taken when drifting. The income of five-man boat fishermen was determined on a share basis but the system differed from community to community. At Staithes and Runswick the gross earnings of a lugger which had gone lining would be divided into six and a half parts. One share went to the owner, one each to the principal five members of the crew — hence the name 'five-man boats' — while the sixth member, who contributed no gear, received a half share. Therefore, if the owner was a crew member he received two shares. If there was more than one owner — which was usually the case — that share would be split between them.[9] The last member of the crew, usually a boy, relied

12

on the generosity of the crew for his reward. At Filey the shares were divided into seven and one given to each of the six men on board.[10] The other share went to the owner. Thus, although the organisation of the fleet of first class fishing vessels was more complex than that for coble operations, the divisions between capital and labour, employer and employed, remained blurred. Most of the crew had capital ventured in the enterprise and their earnings were determined by the craft's success.

The first class fleet was usually fitted out each March to go great lining for white fish, especially large cod, on grounds just off the Dogger Bank. Their normal practice, weather permitting, was to sail on a Monday morning and return with their catch the following Friday. The great lines they laid were also known as 'haavres', a name which may have been derived, according to George Young, from the Swedish word 'haaf', meaning open sea.[11] Being heavier and stronger than the long lines, and carrying larger hooks, they were designed for the capture of 'great fish'. The lines were at least 600 feet long and carried between 90 and 100 hooks attached by snoods. The five main crew members would take three such great lines to sea and they were usually baited at sea with pieces of haddock, herring and other small fish by the boat's lad. Fishing was not carried on from the five-man boat which acted as a kind of floating base, but from cobles, two of which were carried to sea. Since it was important that the amount of time lost through adverse weather conditions was kept to an absolute minimum, it was a great asset that these large luggers were able to lie in extremely heavy seas without running for shelter. Indeed, a Government report of 1849 rated them amongst the most seaworthy fishing craft, in spite of the age of their design.[12] Most of the fish taken during the cod and ling season was landed at Yorkshire coast fishing stations. A substantial portion was taken for curing but much more was shipped off inland. However, the fishermen also took advantage of markets at ports such as Newcastle and Sunderland on the developing north-east coalfield.

As summer drew to a close, the five-man boats were prepared for a six-week voyage to the East Anglian coast to join the autumn herring fishery. They were usually contracted to Great Yarmouth merchants, who not only agreed to take their catch at a fixed rate but also paid them what was known as 'Steerage Money' for the journey south.[13] They followed this fishery until the beginning of

A Typical Yorkshire Lugger (a Staithes five-man boat)
(reproduced by courtesy of the Trustees of the South Kensington Science Museum)

November when they returned home. This basic pattern seems to have changed little from the mid seventeenth century. Upon their return to the Yorkshire coast the vessels were laid up for the winter, mainly in Scarborough and Whitby harbours, until they were refitted next spring for another yearly round. Meanwhile, the fishermen joined the winter inshore coble fishery considered to be the most hazardous of the year's occupations.

As necessary recompense for the levels of capital and labour deployed, the returns from the five-man boat fishery were appreciably higher than those of the coble fishery. Although reliable monthly or annual price statistics for these years have not been uncovered, it is possible to make a crude appraisal of earning potential over their operational year. In 1817 George Young estimated that from each of the luggers about six tons of cod and ling went annually for dry-curing and that the average price obtained by the curers from the London merchants fluctuated between £13 and £30 per ton, with about £18 to £20 being the average.[14] The fishermen, in their turn, often obtained from the curers between £7 and £9 per ton. Taking the lower as the more usual, we arrive at an annual income from this source of around £42 gained during the peak drying months from July to September. However, only about a sixth of the total yearly catch went for dry curing according to George Young. He further estimated that the usual price fishermen obtained over the year for fresh cod and ling was about 18 shillings per score or almost £9 per ton (200 such fish = 1 ton). If we accept Young's estimates on the proportion of fish that were disposed of fresh — on average 30 tons per craft — then a revenue in the region of £270 from this source might be expected in a typical season, or a total of £312 from all white fishing. Furthermore, five-man boats also followed the East Anglian herring fishery and here again George Young supplies us with estimates. According to these, in an average year a boat might take in the region of 30 lasts, each of which would fetch an average of £7 to £8.[15] The possible return from this source, ignoring the highly volatile nature of the herring fisheries, could be in the region of £210. Thus it seems that a three-masted lugger possessed the potential of grossing well over £500 from all sources.

Of course these are crude figures based on the so-called average year and take no account of weekly or even annual fluctuations in price and catch levels. Nevertheless, they do seem broadly accurate for a further assessment of income from white fishing in the pre-railway era claimed earnings of from £12 to £15 in a fair week.[16] This would indicate a total income from six month's white fishing of at least £288.

Over the later eighteenth and early nineteenth centuries there is little evidence to suggest any long-term tendency for the five-man boat fleet to expand or contract markedly. Short term fluctuations were the result of the fortunes of war or through craft being lost on the storm-prone North Sea. When a craft was lost it might not be replaced immediately unless prospects were good, even if the crew were fortunate enough to survive.

The practice of laying up these large craft for about three and a half months each year was partly due to the lack of proper harbour facilities at many of the fishing stations. Furthermore, it was notoriously difficult for sailing craft to enter the three harbour ports during the winter north-easterly gales. Indeed, at first sight it seems remarkable that places such as Flamborough, Staithes and Runswick could operate such craft in safety. The largest fleets of five-man boats were owned by Staithes and Filey. Both overcame their lack of harbour facilities in a number of similar ways. Their fleets were laid up in Scarborough and Whitby harbours during the winter and for part of the year other harbours were utilised. Yarmouth, for example, was the base for the autumn herring fishery. When fishing from their home stations they often remained on the grounds for up to five days before returning towards the weekend to land their catches. Over the weekend they could be moored in Runswick or Filey Bays with comparative safety. In spite of precautions, disaster sometimes struck. One such calamity hit the Filey fleet in 1822. That year two of their craft were dragged from their moorings in a gale and wrecked.[17] That disaster was repeated on a much larger scale in June 1860 when thirteen Filey craft dragged their anchors in a tremendous storm and were lost.[18] In spite of such dangers, the first class fleet continued to flourish.

III

Markets, Products and War, 1780s to the 1810s

Though lining for white fish was the principal catching activity on the Yorkshire coast, other modes of capture were also used. Apart from the small interest in herring drifting, most communities owned a few craft that specialised in taking crabs and lobsters during their seasons. Such pursuits tended to be limited in scope, generally the preserve of the elderly and boys afloat for the first time. Flamborough-caught crabs were held in high regard and hawked around the streets of Scarborough or transported to York and other places on the tops of stage coaches. The turbot or — as it was locally known — bratt fishery was also followed; special stationary nets were laid for the fish on the sea bed. Another minor branch of the fisheries was concerned with the taking of salmon. The Esk was, and indeed still is, an important salmon river; local fishermen caught salmon with nets in June, July and August in the nearby sea. Salmon was highly prized and its captor guaranteed a good market.

Because fish was difficult and expensive to transport overland, inland markets were usually restricted to the wealthier classes; nevertheless, the range of inland trading connections was impressive. As early as the 1770s internal demand was the single most important outlet.[1] Yorkshire coast fish was supplied to numerous inland towns and cities (Fig. 2) including York, Leeds, Bradford, Halifax, Thirsk and Malton. At Thirsk fresh fish was sold on a Monday market held in Low Street, while Fossgate was York's main market for fish, sold there by the panniermen every Wednesday and Friday.[2] By the 1780s Staithes and other communities were even supplying the Manchester market and some of

17

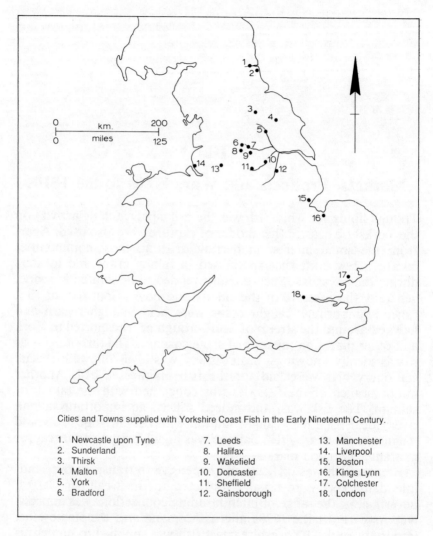

Cities and Towns supplied with Yorkshire Coast Fish in the Early Nineteenth Century.

1. Newcastle upon Tyne	7. Leeds	13. Manchester
2. Sunderland	8. Halifax	14. Liverpool
3. Thirsk	9. Wakefield	15. Boston
4. Malton	10. Doncaster	16. Kings Lynn
5. York	11. Sheffield	17. Colchester
6. Bradford	12. Gainsborough	18. London

Figure 2.

Cities and Towns supplied with Yorkshire Coast Fish in the Early Nineteenth Century.

Sources: PRO, Cust. 91/116; *Hull Advertiser,* 1794-1820.

this fish found its way to Liverpool.[3] However, these markets were again restricted to the more affluent, for as late as 1841 fish was not normally within the range of the Manchester working-class diet.

An increasing quantity of fish was also carried along the tributaries of the River Humber during those years; Hull had long been an important market for fish landed on the coast and was also the distributive centre for the river trade.[4] Fish was also carried up and down the coast to various ports between Newcastle and London.[5]

The export trade, also regarded as a valuable outlet, was chiefly in dried fish and locally cured cod had a good reputation overseas. Although the West Indies and Ireland were sometimes supplied, the most important export markets in terms of quality and value were northern Spain and the Mediterranean states. In 1820, Bilbao, Santander, Corunna and San Sebastian took 2526 cwt and such outlets had been important elements of the Yorkshire coast trade since at least the first half of the eighteenth century. Although other fishing regions tried to secure a foothold in these markets, none could match the expertise of the Yorkshire curers. Some fish was directly exported to Spain but the bulk was sent coastwise to London and then forwarded overseas by reputable merchants whose names guaranteed quality. These trading connections were very strong and many of the Yorkshire coast curers contracted to sell their fish to London merchants before each drying season. Yorkshire's dominance of the prime export markets was due to a combination of factors, both natural and human. In England a number of areas, including the south west, East Anglia and Northumberland, cured fish in the same fashion but none could match the Yorkshire output. North of the border the story was somewhat different. The output of Shetland, for example, was much greater than that of the Yorkshire coast in terms of quantity but fell below it in quality. In part this was due to the damper climatic conditions which impeded the drying processes, and in part because of the higher curing standards adopted by the Yorkshiremen.[6]

Virtually every coastal community from Flamborough northwards dry-cured fish and the techniques adopted by the Yorkshire curers were quite complex. After being caught, split and salted, the fish were spread out on rocks on the beach and nearby hills until apparently dry. They were then gathered into a large pile and left to stand for ten to twelve days; this part of the process was known as sweating. Then the stack was opened out, sorted and the fish exposed again to the sun and air. After this last stage of the drying process the fish were packed into 5lb parcels for forwarding to the merchants. Cod and ling were the principal varieties cured in this fashion but coal fish and skate were similarly processed for the home market; skate dried to the consistency of horn was a speciality unique to Filey curers.[7] Because of the importance of climatic conditions, this form of curing could be carried on only during the summer months and activity along the Yorkshire coast reached its peak between July and September. Almost every spare pair of hands was employed in turning the fish or guarding it from sea birds. At Staithes this drying harvest covered all available ground, while at Robin Hood's Bay in the 1790s many house fronts were covered with hanging fish and others were spread over the neighbouring paddocks.[8] Such sights can scarcely have been attractive to the fashionable visitor yet the practice was part and parcel of life even at the growing resorts of Filey and Scarborough; indeed, Scarborough's outer pier was rented out for this purpose in later years.[9]

Each community usually had more than one curer although their numbers fluctuated; Staithes, the most important centre, was sometimes the base for four or five, and though it was usually a male-dominated occupation, women sometimes conducted curing operations, notably Mary Potter who worked at Scarborough in the early decades of the nineteenth century. The scale of an individual curing concern can be gauged from Table 2 which shows the output of Christopher Moore who worked at both Staithes and Runswick. The table presents data for 1820 which seem typical of individual curing activities over the previous forty or so years. The curers also supplemented their income by producing substantial quantities of cod liver oil which was sent along the coast to places such as Hull and London.

The circumscribed nature of the herring fishery is perhaps the most surprising feature of the late eighteenth and early nineteenth centuries. In spite of the appearance of huge shoals between July and September little interest was shown and the market for those herrings landed was limited, even though the fishery had been of considerable importance in earlier centuries. These shoals were sometimes pursued with greater vigour at times of acute wartime food shortages,[10] but such interest was not sustained, even though

Yorkshire fishermen still followed the East Anglian autumn herring fishery. It seems that lining for white fish was the more attractive summer proposition.

Table 2

Fish Cured at Staithes and Runswick Bay by Christopher Moore

	Dry Cured cwts		Pickle Cured barrels
Staithes			
1820		1820	
Aug. 25	165½	Dec. 7	29
Sept. 2	6	Dec. 15	26
Oct. 4	60	Dec. 18	5
Oct. 25	111¾	1821	
Total	343¼	Jan. 13	41½
		Jan. 15	7
		Feb. 1	32
		Total	140½
Runswick			
1820		1820	
Sept. 9	189	Dec. 14	24½
Total	189	Dec. 20	10
		1821	
		Jan. 13	36½
		Feb. 1	1
		Total	72
Grand Totals			
Dry Cured	532¼	**Pickle Cured**	212½

Source: RHE, AF1/5 22 May 1821

Although the fisheries off the Yorkshire coast were worked on a far greater scale than has sometimes been suggested, by a local industry of considerable sophistication, there was still considerable scope for expansion, as the experience of later years would demonstrate. The evidence available suggests that the late eighteenth and early nineteenth centuries were not times of dynamic growth for the Yorkshire coast fishing industry; nor were they notable for the adoption of any new techniques or practices. Some growth may have occurred over the second half of the eighteenth century but if so it was undramatic. National population growth does not seem to have stimulated changes on the scale of those being wrought in agriculture. To understand the reasons for this lack of development it is necessary to look first at the marketing and distributive sectors of the industry.

During the whole of this time, and long before, the fishing industry had been restricted by transportation problems. Distribution of fish was hampered by the relatively high cost and slow pace of most existing forms of transport. Although all economic activities were affected to varying degrees by the same problems, the situation was particularly acute for the fishing industry since its products were often highly perishable. Fish deteriorated so rapidly that it could only be kept for any length of time by being heavily cured. This markedly restricted the product range that could be placed before the inland consumer. During years of poor harvests fish could often have satisfied the hunger of the poor had it not been for the problem of transporting it from the quayside. A tragic example of this inability to overcome the bottleneck occurred during the winter of 1766/7. That season Scarborough fishermen located immense shoals of haddock which continued in roe until the middle of February. Many cobles were deployed and the quantities landed each day were so great that the market was overwhelmed and the poor were able to buy the smaller sort for 1*d* or 1½*d* a score. But the quantities landed sometimes exceeded local demand and fishermen were obliged to lay up their cobles for a time. While local towns and villages benefited from this surfeit, the rest of the country was subject to great dearth and the poor were in such distress 'that dangerous insurrections were excited and many families were perishing through want of food'.[11]

The crux of the problem was that, although it was possible to get fish to market in a relatively fresh state by means of pannier trains and carts, the cost limited such trade to the higher end of the market. The inland poor could not normally afford quality fresh fish but along the Yorkshire, East Anglian and Devon coasts, where it was in ample supply, it was a regular and accepted part of local diet. It has been suggested that the inland fish trade was restricted because the poor considered fish an inferior food and there is a great deal of contemporary evidence which suggests that the poor did not like the *type* of fish they were offered. Quality fresh fish was certainly enjoyed by those who could afford it. Defoe, on his travels around the country in the 1720s seems almost to lick his lips when describing the range of fish available at ports such as Scarborough[12] and such fare was always prominently mentioned in Yorkshire coast visitors' guide books of the late eighteenth and early nineteenth centuries. Away from the coast the only fish that the poor could afford for much of the year was that originally intended for the richer consumer which had begun to turn. Such a situation had long existed: fish condemned at seventeenth century Billingsgate found poorer outlets elsewhere.[13] Such practices could still be noted by an observer in 1817: 'When the poor obtain fish, it is generally half rotten and consequently most unwholesome and disgusting food'.[14]

There was, however, one type of fish destined for consumption by the poor — the herring. They might be eaten in cured form although large quantities were retailed in varying degrees of freshness at many urban communities within reach. Herrings were caught in such large numbers that they could be moved in bulk by boat or cart and thus sold cheaply, but they deteriorated much more swiftly than white fish if not processed. Without curing, decay would set in within a day or two so that fish moved from East Anglia to London by boat often must have begun to turn on arrival. It is not surprising, then, that although herrings were eaten in great quantities because of their cheapness they were hardly regarded by the eighteenth-century London poor in anything but an inferior light.[15] The obvious course of action was to cure the fish but once more the problem was the quality of the product reaching the poorer consumer. Heavy methods of curing were needed in the absence of other forms of storage or preservation. The three principal modes of English curing were salt pickling in barrels, smoking for up to three weeks, or drying by air or wind. However, processing standards were extremely variable. Indeed, it was a notorious fact that one reason for the British inability to compete with the Dutch in overseas' markets was that curing standards were so inferior. Where quality could be ensured — as with some Yorkshire coast cured cod — then demand was firm. Other cured fish was treated with much more reserve by all classes.

The curers also found it difficult to respond effectively to sudden surges in demand perhaps occasioned by a dearth of other provisions.[16] Smokehouse production of red herrings and the like — under which a fish might be processed for up to twenty-one days — could not be swiftly increased unless short-cuts were taken which led to a less thoroughly cured and second-rate product. More importantly perhaps, supplies of salt for curing could not be obtained swiftly. Although saltworks were to be found at several locations in Britain, the only native supply suitable for curing fish came from Cheshire. This was usually forwarded by canal to Liverpool and then dispatched by sea around the coast and considerable time could elapse between ordering and delivery. Moreover, curers were unlikely to hoard large quantities of salt in readiness for any possible surge in demand because of the Salt Laws; after 1786 salt curers were exempted from salt tax but had to adhere to strict regulations in order to prevent fraudulent use. These involved the costly construction of a bonded warehouse and the need to invest considerable capital reduced the incentive to hold extra supplies.

Hull, like many towns, was anxious to increase the supply of fish it received and at least as early as 1772 introduced a series of financial incentives — known as bounties — for fishermen who supplied its market. These were later refined and extended and lasted until at least 1807.[17] Hull was by no means alone in such positive endeavours. Indeed, the Government involved itself closely in the development of voluntary schemes and in 1801 — in response to acute wartime provisioning problems — empowered the Treasury to introduce a bounty system for fish brought to key ports around the British coast. These moves were perhaps marginally successful in that they increased supplies to centres offering the bounties but probably at the expense of other markets that lacked such incentives. Bad harvests and the disruption of overseas sources of supplies due to the French Wars were the principal reasons for this acute interest in the provisioning problem; like later conflagrations, these wars had an effect on the fishing industry that was disruptive and yet stimulating. The shifting quicksand of military alliances played havoc with normal channels of trade and no sector was more affected than exports of cured fish from the Yorkshire coast to southern European markets. The regular trade with Spain evaporated in 1796[18] and although some exports found their way to north European ports such as Hamburg[19] these outlets were in turn lost as the course of the war took other twists. On the credit side, however, such problems did not in themselves prove catastrophic because of the chronic home shortage of other provisions. In short, a buoyant English demand for fish more than compensated for the loss of overseas markets.

The most obvious problem for fishermen was that, as always, they were in the front line of the maritime conflict. The massive expansion of the Royal Navy's strength meant that the press-gang was increasingly used and, although many landsmen were sucked into the Navy, the main aim was to recruit skilled sailors who were a prime asset for any fighting ship. The situation of the fishermen was somewhat ambiguous. As expert seamen they were obviously attractive to the Royal Navy, and the reservoir of maritime skills contained amongst their ranks had long been used as an argument as to why the Government should stimulate the development of the fisheries. Even the arch free trader Adam Smith conceded that there might be some validity in this point.[20] However, as in previous conflicts many groups of fishermen were protected from the press-gang by special dispensations.[21] Immunity was usually granted so that fish supplies could be maintained and any general provisioning shortage not aggravated. But, in reality, the press-gang sometimes paid scant regard to the regulations and during the 1790s one group was especially vigorous in its attentions to the Yorkshire coast, roaming the entire seaboard from the Tyne to the Humber. The hostility which its activities attracted provoked a riot at Whitby in 1793, and the customary practice of women in communities such as Robin Hood's Bay on the approach of the press-gang was to beat and rattle a drum to warn their men to keep clear.[22] Nevertheless, by one means or another, many fishermen were recruited into the Navy and nowhere was this more evident than at Staithes; in 1813 the number of cobles licensed was down to 42, yet by 1816, when the de-commissioning of His Majesty's ships was well underway, the figure leapt up to 67.[23]

The fishermen who managed to avoid the press-gang or chose not to join up of their own accord were still likely to face the enemy in the course of their normal day to day activities. During the 1790s, and for much of the following decade, privateers were an ever-present threat. Indeed, the North Sea was reported to be infested with them early in 1801.[24] These were generally heavily-armed three-masted luggers that cruised the shipping lanes in search of lone vessels such as colliers or Baltic convoy stragglers they could capture as prizes. Fishing boats, even the larger ones, with no cargo other than their catch were less obvious targets but the relationship they enjoyed with the enemy was never better than uneasy. In previous conflicts there was a long catalogue of fishing vessels taken by the enemy: both Scarborough and Whitby had lost craft to the Dutch in 1649.[25] In the later eighteenth century they were less obvious targets although some craft still fell victim. During the French Wars fishing vessels were treated differently from merchant ships, which were always considered legitimate targets by both sides, yet their position was never entirely secure, for their treatment was subject both to shifts in military policy and to the whim of the individual privateer.

Relations between the fishermen and privateers were particularly variable. For much of the time they ignored each other although on some occasions encounters of an apparently friendlier nature occurred. There was a number of incidents similar to the one which took place off the Humber in March 1801 when the master of a French privateer regaled the crew of a fishing boat with spirits in return for a little of their catch;[26] perhaps this was an attempt to gain information on shipping movements as well as fresh food. On other occasions, contacts were more hostile; during the summer of 1794 fishing operations on the Dogger Bank had to be suspended for a time because of harrassment by French privateers and on a number of occasions craft were chased and caught. Not all violent encounters were to the detriment of the fishermen. In late 1794 fishermen from Filey were able to retake a British brig laden with corn from Emden that had been captured by a French privateer; the vessel, with a prize crew of four, was driven by adverse weather conditions into Filey Bay and this gave the fishermen the opportunity to overwhelm the privateers.[27] In August 1797 a small privateer carrying four guns and a crew of between twenty and twenty-five chased one of the Scarborough five-man boats right up to the harbour. After failing in this pursuit it turned towards Filey Bay, but hunter became hunted as the five-man boat swiftly took on board arms and extra crew and set off in pursuit of the privateer. When the enemy vessel was encountered a fierce fight ensued during which it was overpowered and brought into Scarborough harbour.[28] Over the entire period from 1793 to 1815 the five-man boat fleet was remarkably lucky; a survey of vessels registered at Whitby, Scarborough and Bridlington Custom Houses reveals that none was taken by privateers, even though there were numerous reports of merchant vessel losses. An important factor may have been their speed, for being three-masted luggers they were probably amongst the few craft that could outrun many privateers. Such a course of action was not, however, without cost for if the boat had its gear out when a privateer bore down on it the warps had to be cut and expensive nets or lines abandoned.

The fluctuations in the size of the first class fishing fleet's strength were due to the course of the war. The decline in the labour force available tended to be reflected at times in the number of craft operating. However, the prosperity induced by the high price of provisions during the early 1800s encouraged a spate of five-man boat construction, but as the total labour force available was still shrinking, such expansion was probably at the expense of the coble fishery.

Food was again in short supply during the years 1811 to 1813 and the resultant high price of fish provoked much comment both nationally and locally. By 1813 Scarborough was suffering from a shortage of fish since so much of the local catch was being forwarded to other markets without being offered for sale in the town. The resort's burghers appealed for ideas to divert this flow of fish back to their own market. A couple of schemes were put forward to prevent the outflow, the most ambitious of which proposed the setting up of a company under the patronage of the corporation with a capital of £2000. This concern was to undertake the curing and sale of fish and, presumably, gain control of the fish supply by operating its own boats, and all fish was to be offered for sale for two hours in the town's markets before any could be sent inland.[29]

The return of peace which followed the exile of Napoleon to St Helena in 1815 saw a return to the old patterns of activity: export

27

links with Spain and the Mediterranean were soon restored and with the demobilisation of the Navy the fishing industry's labour force regained its strength. In spite of the massive wartime upheaval it is remarkable how traditional patterns of activity reasserted themselves. Exploitation of the herring fishery fell back to its previous low level, line fishing continued to be the dominant interest, and the strength of the first class fishing fleet was soon very similar to what it had been in the later 1780s. The long term trends, therefore, emphasised continuity and stability. No permanent changes can be noted that could be compared, for example, with the great upsurge of enclosures that had been such a feature of wartime agriculture. It seems likely that the crucial catalyst for change was still trapped within bottlenecks on the distributive side.

IV

New Developments 1815-1840

The years immediately following the Napoleonic Wars were prosperous ones for the Yorkshire coast fishing industry and there was a vigorous spate of renewal and replacement among the five-man boat fleet. The great dearth of 1816 raised fish prices along with other foodstuffs and fishermen seem to have benefited from the continuation of local provisioning problems that lasted — albeit intermittently — until at least 1821; over the five years ending 1820 some twenty-one first class fishing craft were constructed for the communities of Filey, Scarborough, Robin Hood's Bay, Runswick and Staithes. Initially, Scarborough took the lead with five vessels registered in 1815 alone. Most boats built during those years were turned out in Scarborough harbour by the builder John Skelton, but by the end of the decade his production was largely for Staithes.[1] This prosperity was matched by the open boat fishery and a large number of new cobles was licensed, particularly over the years 1816-18.

In 1820 the Government introduced new financial incentives in an attempt to increase exports of cured fish. Since 1808 bounties had been granted on herring cured to a standard laid down by a newly-created body called the Herring Fishery Commissioners. This Treasury-financed organisation had created a network of inspection points and appointed experienced former curers as its officers. These men were charged with overseeing curing processes and the granting of bounties on barrels of herring processed to the requisite standard. In the long term this policy proved a marked success for it helped establish the Scottish herring trade's reputation, which was followed by a marked expansion of production

29

and exports over the nineteenth century. From 1820 the same system was applied to the cod, ling and hake fisheries. The Edinburgh based Fishery Commissioners were firstly empowered to pay a bounty of up to 50s. per ton on all decked vessels fitting out for those fisheries in an agreed fashion. All dried fish cured to a requisite standard was marked with a specially designed punch which made a hole in their tail and granted a bounty of 4s. per cwt. Pickle cured fish entitled to the bounty had their barrels branded with a mark of approval in a similar fashion to that already applied in the herring fishery and for a time all non-approved fish was barred from exportation.

This attempt to expand the fisheries met with little success on the Yorkshire coast. In 1820, the last full year prior to the introduction of these bounties, some 5474 cwt of dried and 448 barrels of salt-pickled cod and ling were produced. During the following nine years when the bounty operated the former figure was surpassed only once and the latter never even remotely approached. Indeed, overall production trends were downwards with an annual average output of 4640 cwt of dried cod and ling being recorded for the years 1821-5 which fell to 3842 cwt for the following five years. Production of salt-pickled cod and ling shrivelled to almost nothing.[2] This downturn was apparently general across the fishery for in spite of the financial cushion offered by the bounty, the first class fleet contracted markedly over the first half of the decade. Nowhere was this more apparent than in the more southerly stations with the number of five-man boats registered at Scarborough Custom House falling from twenty to twelve in just five years. Although this decline was halted over the second half of the decade there were few signs of recovery. This catalogue of decline on the Yorkshire coast was at variance with a national picture of growth.[3] Its problems do not appear to be related to catching difficulties — surviving records make no reference to poor catches — but these regional difficulties may have been exacerbated by expansion in other areas and the subsequent increase in competition.

However, it cannot be said that the work of the Fishery Commissioners on the Yorkshire coast was a total failure, for they managed to bring about some improvements in the methods of dry curing, even though the local curers already had a considerable reputation. Nevertheless, the London merchants who exported the fish felt that many possible sales were lost through variations in the quality of the finished product. The most common faults included differences in the thoroughness of drying. In part this was unavoidable due to climatic changeability, but it was often the result of poor curing techniques or the haste of a processor to increase turnover at times when demand was high. Occasionally the possibility of greater gain might tempt a curer to be more devious, as was the case with a Flamborough individual who was found to be mixing poor quality fish with good in an attempt to secure the highest price for all.[4] Other fish could be spoilt by excessive drying and quality was also affected by over-exposure to strong sun which resulted in blistering. Some fish lost value through being 'salt burnt', which was caused by the application of too much salt after splitting. Poor storage and damp conditions could turn even well-cured fish mouldy and this problem ruined the entire stock of one reputable Scarborough curer in 1822.[5] Sea voyages could also have a detrimental effect on quality. In order to eradicate, or at least minimise, the effect of these shortcomings a complex series of regulations was drawn up by the Fishery Commissioners and these had to be closely adhered to by both fishermen and curers if they wished to claim the bounty. All curing processes were overseen by their officer and only those cured fish he inspected and passed received the punch mark in the tail from his special iron.

The first district officer appointed to the Yorkshire coast was a Scotsman, George Smith, and his strict implementation of the regulations soon produced a whole spate of complaints from local curers to his Edinburgh superiors. His stand was firmly backed by the Fishery Commissioners and even Smith himself was severely reprimanded when he allowed the bounty on some fish not cured in a manner wholly in accordance with regulations.[6] These efforts were rewarded with considerable success. In 1823 the London Officer of the Fishery Commissioners, Archibald Cameron, commented on the considerable overall improvement in the quality of curing and a similar state of affairs was reported by the Secretary when he visited the area in 1825. In practical terms this meant that more of the dried fish could be sold to Spanish markets and less had to be disposed of in the lower value Irish or West Indian markets. This was appreciated by the curers who conveyed to the Secretary 'the most unqualified testimony of the utility of the regulations issued by the Commissioners, and of the great improvement thereby effected in the quality of the fish'.[7]

In another respect, however, the work of the Fishery Commissioners was probably to the disadvantage of the Yorkshire coast, for although they improved the quality of curing they also raised standards elsewhere, particularly in the later 1820s; between 1825 and 1829 the quantity of fish cured nationally that reached bounty standard rose from 52,135 cwt to 92,124 cwt.[8] There were still regional variations in quality that left the Yorkshire coast to the forefront but the general adoption of the regulations had the effect of narrowing the gap. This marked increase in the supply of high quality cured fish lowered prices overall. Furthermore, many Scottish districts had lower production costs and there are numerous instances of English craft finding it cheaper to buy fish from Scottish fishermen rather than catch it themselves. Such factors probably account for the fall off in Yorkshire coast output at that time.

Nevertheless, throughout the 1820s, the Yorkshire coast was able to maintain its position as the largest producer of dried cod and ling in England, even though its output was dwarfed by that of Shetland; as early as 1821 Shetland turned out 29,301 cwt of punched fish compared with the Yorkshire coast total of 5623 cwt. However, the impressive Shetland figures reflect the lack of other outlets whereas only one-sixth of the Yorkshire catch went for dry curing with the rest finding sales inland. Data to back up these assertions do not become available until 1842 by which time Yorkshire dry curing activities were on the decline. Even so, they illustrate the difference in the relative size of other outlets, for in that year cod and ling sold for purposes other than curing in the Yorkshire and Shetland districts totalled 27,996 cwt and 3563 cwt respectively.

In the mid 1820s Government fisheries policy began to shift once more. The Salt Laws, long regarded as being to the detriment of the industry, were repealed and from 1825 all fishing bounties were gradually phased out. Although the oversight of curing by the Fishery Commissioners continued, the financial incentives they provided ceased at the end of the decade. The move was viewed with alarm in Yorkshire, especially as the industry was experiencing difficult times. Fishermen and curers from Staithes to Flamborough petitioned Parliament on five separate occasions

32

praying for the continuance of the bounty system;[9] other districts adopted the same tactic but all efforts proved to be in vain and the subsidies ceased as scheduled at the end of 1829.

The complete removal of financial assistance did not turn out to be the disaster that the Yorkshire industry had feared. Not only did it almost coincide with an upturn in home demand that was a feature of the 1830s but the end of bounties seems to have benefited the area at the expense of other districts. In Shetland the move was little short of calamitous and prompted a collapse in dry curing activity; craft were laid up and left to rot on the shore[10] and for a while all interest in the Fishery Commissioners' curing regulations was lost. Yet on the Yorkshire coast, the amount of fish dry cured rose. Furthermore, the district was able to strengthen its position in the quality overseas trade as the challenge from Shetland and other areas receded. Indeed, the quality gap between Yorkshire curers and their rivals was, if anything, wider than ever before. Most other areas abandoned the official dry curing regulations once the bounty was removed while the Yorkshire curers continued to follow them and have their fish stamped with the punch of approval.

In spite of the resurgence in dry curing activity, the primary stimulant to growth on the Yorkshire coast during the 1830s came from an expansion of the home market. The growing northern industrial areas provided markets for the fish trade that were limited only by the constraints of existing modes of transportation. The practice of landing at seaports outside of the area also proved more lucrative. Coastwise trade was also speeded up by the arrival of the steam packets which established a number of services along the east coast during the early thirties. These vessels could take consignments of fish from ports such as Whitby and Scarborough and deliver them quite swiftly to the quaysides of Hull, Hartlepool, Newcastle or places even further afield. Steam packets were also making an impact on trading along the Humber waterway system.[11] Hull had long been both an important market and redistributive centre for fish. The quaysides near the present Minerva tavern were the scene of ever more vigorous activity during the 1830s, which provoked numerous complaints from local residents about the nuisances associated with the trade,[12] as the fish was transferred into river craft. The arrival of steam packets was of particular importance to fish traffic for they enabled consignments to reach towns on the Humber's tributaries much more swiftly, leaving less time for deterioration. This proved an important factor in the development of the Yorkshire coast herring fishery. There had been some native exploitation of the fishery for centuries, with a few craft supplying local demand, but the shoals had been left largely to the Dutch. This situation began to change about 1824 when the French began to visit the coast in growing numbers; they had been operating off Yarmouth as early as 1819 and were eventually to spread their efforts along the entire British North Sea coast.[13] Though sometimes a source of intense irritation to local fishermen, because their heavy gear occasionally damaged the nets and lines of others, they also encouraged greater native participation, for their large boats — often with a crew of about thirty — came not only to catch fish in their own right but also to buy and cure them. Many acted as factory ships carrying their own barrels and salt, and processed herring acquired from local fishermen.[14] By the early 1830s the French presence was considerable; more than a hundred of their craft were noted in the vicinity of Saltburn Bay on one day alone during the summer of 1834. To a certain degree they took the position of the Dutch who appeared in ever-diminishing numbers. As Yorkshiremen turned to supplying the French with herring they soon found there was competition for their catches. English merchants quickly recognised the potential of this fishery and by the mid 1830s most complaints about French fishing activities came from their ranks. Their interest was perhaps less for the welfare of the fishermen than from the fact that the French were rival purchasers of catches.

The development of the herring fishery was assisted by the appointment of a new district officer of the Fishery Commissioners in 1830. He was Donald MacLaren who, having been stationed previously at Yarmouth, was undoubtedly conversant with all aspects of the herring trade, and his advice proved useful to local individuals embarking upon the business for the first time. Expansion of the shore-based side of this fishery really took off in the autumn of 1833 with the formation of the Whitby Herring Company,[15] a venture promoted by fourteen local tradespeople whose traditional areas of interest in whaling and shipbuilding were in marked decline.[16] They thus had every incentive to seek a new outlet for their enterprise. Within the space of a few months the company had erected smokehouses and curing yards in the Tait Hill area of the town and many of the herrings cured were sold to vessels from France and Belgium. The firm's prosperity was enhanced as the decade wore on. In just one week during the September of 1839 it took 120 lasts of herrings for curing and purchased a further 50 tons for dispatch mainly in an uncured state to inland markets. As outlets increased more craft were attracted and as early as the summer of 1834 Whitby harbour was reported to be busier than ever before with numerous boats, yawls and cobles landing their catches on the quays. These craft were attracted from as far afield as Cromer, Hastings and Yarmouth, and by the 1836 season some 400 craft were reported to be employed in fishing for herring off the Yorkshire coast.[17]

Whitby harbour was not alone in playing host to the herring fishermen. Considerable activity was soon noted at Scarborough and Staithes was also to benefit. Scarborough's early interest in the trade was in supplying salt-cured herrings to overseas markets, but home demand became increasingly important and by the early 1840s assumed the dominant position. Some of the fish destined for the English markets was cured in a smokehouse erected at the foot of Oliver's Mount.[18] An indication of the marked effect that the resurgence of the herring trade had on local fishing communities can be gleaned from a survey of Custom House records for the period. Prior to 1833, only cobles and five-man boats were listed in the registers but in the July of that year a new type of craft made an appearance.[19] This departure from traditional design was named *Integrity* and was constructed by Robert Skelton, the Scarborough boatbuilder. Skelton built the craft as a speculation — in other words he had no order for her — and he derived the design from Cromer and Cley craft that were visiting the area to supply the French with herring. He believed that there could be a local demand for such craft, once they had proved their worth to local fishermen. During the first year of operations Skelton retained the bulk of the shares in the vessel with only one quarter being held by a local fisherman, Thomas Race, who skippered her. *Integrity* was somewhat smaller than the five-man boats, measuring just over 34 feet from stem to stern. She carried just two masts and was only partially decked, and had a narrow rather than a square stern like the larger craft.

Integrity's success is apparent from the flood of orders for similar craft that came Skelton's way over the following years. In 1834 he sold his interest in her and concentrated on building new and improved versions; in that year alone ten were constructed for Filey and Scarborough fishermen followed by five in the next.[20] Later in the decade a couple were built for Staithes and Robin Hood's Bay, but until the 1850s these craft were mainly concentrated further south. Skelton and other builders continued to refine and improve on this class of craft which became known as Yorkshire yawls. By the end of the 1830s newly-turned-out yawls were fully decked craft of considerably larger size and the narrow stern had been superceded by one similar to that found on the five-man boats. As with cobles, each boatbuilder's design differed in detail, which was only to be expected in craft built by the eye rather than blueprint. The yawl's principal advantages over the five-man boats were those of being cheaper to construct and needing a smaller crew.[21] They were soon following the same annual round of activity as the larger craft. Such developments were echoed in the open boat fishery. In 1834 new types of undecked vessels appear in the Whitby Register of Boat Licenses. These were longer than the coble and had the advantage of being able to carry more nets to sea.[22] They were built specifically for the herring fishery and were forerunners of the craft known as mules and ploshers. When the season ended they were laid up on the shore and their crews returned to the cobles for the line fishery. Such extra vessels meant a considerable increase in capital investment per crew which is indicative of the prosperity which the herring fishery brought.

A further result of the resurgence of the herring fishery was Whitby's re-emergence as a notable fishing station. Not only did the port act as host to visiting herring craft but it also attracted fishing families from the surrounding communities of Runswick and Robin Hood's Bay[23] who built up an interest in the open boat line fishery. An additional attraction was undoubtedly provided by the opening of the horse-drawn Whitby to Pickering Railway in 1836 which was carrying appreciable loads of fish by early in the following decade.

Other evidence of growing marketing opportunities during the 1830s can be found in the visits of trawling smacks during the summer season. These arrivals concentrated on supplying the fashionable resort of Scarborough and seem to have filled a niche in the market left vacant by local concentration on the herring or inland white fish trade. In fact, such a wealth of opportunities presented themselves during this decade that dry curing activities were somewhat neglected when all other factors should have encouraged growth. Although output increased it fell behind demand and as early as 1831 the Fishery Commissioners were bemoaning the shortfall in supply of quality cured cod and ling of the type the Yorkshire coast was noted for. The following year considerable quantities were shipped direct to Spain and such was the demand that some Spanish merchants came to the Yorkshire coast to purchase their fish straight from the curers. Because the output of Yorkshire dry cured fish was insufficient to satisfy those markets the London merchants looked once more for other sources of supply. In 1837 the firm of Hay and Ogilvie decided to try to sell the Shetland product on the Spanish market again. In an attempt to induce the curers there to adopt the 'Yorkshire Method' of curing, they arranged for Archibald Cameron, the London Officer of the Fishery Commissioners, to visit the islands.[24] A combination of effort by all concerned over the next two seasons produced Shetland fish of a standard acceptable for the Spanish and Mediterranean markets.

Such increased supply had a downward effect on prices at the quality end of the market, and this was particularly evident by 1839 when the highest price offered to Yorkshire curers was only £16 per ton compared with £18 and £19 the year before.[25] Yet unlike in Shetland, where there were few other outlets for the catch, it was difficult to cut costs. If curers reduced the price they offered for fish then the Yorkshire fishermen could turn to other outlets which were becoming increasingly available. Thus by the end of the decade the Yorkshire coast dry curing sector found itself caught between conflicting economic forces that bore ill for its continued vitality.

In contrast to the previous decade, the 1830s brought increased opportunity and growth to the Yorkshire coast fishing industry. This was reflected particularly by a marked expansion in the strength of the labour force and in the size of the first class fleet. It adds weight to the contention that the whole period from the Napoleonic Wars to the 1840s was one of expansion for the English fishing industry. Nevertheless, the experience of the area during the 1820s shows that such growth was by no means even;

37

how far the stagnation and decline of that decade were purely local
features will only be established after more regional research.

V

Railways and the Rise of Trawling

The four decades following 1840 witnessed a great expansion in the country's fishing industry. The construction of the national railway network led to the breaking of the transport bottleneck that had long constrained the trade and ultimately provided the means of making fish an article of cheap mass consumption. Yet this potential was not realised overnight. In 1840 the concept of transport by rail was still in its infancy and much was still to be learnt about the problems associated with reaching national agreements on carriage rates and operating conditions for all types of traffic. Though the level of rail-borne traffic grew during the ensuing decade, it was not until the 1850s that nationally acceptable fish carriage policies emerged which allowed a massive expansion of the trade.

The first rail link to a Yorkshire port had been established as early as 1830 when the Stockton to Darlington line was extended to the hamlet of Middlesbrough which soon became a bustling centre of maritime commerce. However, that undertaking was primarily for the export of coal, and its early trade links were largely with the collieries of south west Durham so it was of only limited use to the fishing industry of the period. It was followed by the construction of the Whitby to Pickering Railway which became fully operational by early July 1836, a venture which was to prove of early benefit to the fish trade. Until 1845 the line's motive power was provided by a combination of stationary engine and horses so that although fish trains travelled at five miles an hour,[1] their advantage over pannier ponies was less dramatic than if steam locomotives had been employed. Moreover, any fish destined for

39

markets further afield had to be transferred back to conventional transport at Pickering since before the mid 1840s this railway was isolated from developments taking place elsewhere: the nearest rail connection was at York, a full thirty miles away. In spite of such disadvantages, the fish trade found this new mode of transport useful. In August 1839 when the fishery was in full swing, the *Eastern Counties Herald* noted that an immense quantity of herrings was being sent up the line.[2] The surviving traffic receipts for the half year July-December 1843 show that fish was the second most valuable source of goods income, exceeded only by stone; 714 tons of fish were conveyed realising an income of £302 6s 3d. or over a quarter of the total goods traffic revenue.[3] However, the railway cannot be regarded as the stimulus which triggered the growth of the herring fishery since growth began prior to its opening and the fishery expanded at all centres along the Yorkshire coast and not just at Whitby.

Yorkshire's first direct rail link between the North Sea and the growing industrial centres grouped around the Pennines was forged in 1840 with the opening of the Hull and Selby Railway. Thereafter, merchandise could be conveyed via the York and North Midland Railway or the Manchester and Leeds Railway to a whole range of towns. Within another decade the port of Hull came to possess railway connections with most major English towns. But this enterprise was of only limited direct benefit to the established fishing industry since Hull did not possess a sizeable fishing fleet at that time. However, fishing vessels from both Yorkshire and further south had been in the habit of making landings at the port both to supply its growing population and to take advantage of the network of inland communications based on the Humber and its tributaries. Other fish had long been forwarded to the town by boat or cart. Once the railway was opened, the logical step was to use Hull to send fish to inland markets, but at first such traffic was insignificant. Then, in the spring of 1841, the boards of the Manchester and Leeds, Leeds and Selby Railways, together with the Hull and Selby Railway Company reached agreement on a scheme to encourage through traffic. It was arranged that receipts should be divided in proportion to the route mileage of each concern that the traffic travelled over. Early in the following year the scheme was extended to encourage the development of through fish traffic. Captain James Laws, manager of the

Manchester and Leeds Railway, was the moving force. After negotiating with the managements of the various railway companies and the fishermen of Filey and Flamborough, he was able to secure the introduction of a more attractive and cheaper range of carriage rates and conditions of travel.[4] These made it worthwhile for the fish trade to send cheaper grades of fresh fish long distances overland for the first time. Captain Laws arranged for an area of land to be set aside in Manchester by the Salford side of Victoria Bridge and a number of individuals from the fishing communities concerned opened a shop-cum-stall under the name of the Flamborough and Filey Bay Fishing Company. Arrangements for forwarding the fish were complex and the time-table tight. Fish, landed at Bridlington Quay, Flamborough or Filey in the afternoon, was conveyed in carts over the thirty or more miles to Hull whence it was forwarded by rail at six o'clock the following morning. Manchester was generally reached at noon so that the fish could be placed on sale within twenty-four hours of landing. In poor weather conditions this timetable could not always be met and arrangements were made for the fish to leave Hull on the eight o'clock train and arrive at Manchester by two in the afternoon.[5]

The shop, which opened for the first time on the last Saturday of January 1842, usually received a fresh supply of fish every day except Sunday. The scheme soon proved a resounding success. Fresh fish was on offer in Manchester as low as 1¼d. per lb, whereas previously it was rare if it fell as low as 8d. per lb. Demand was overwhelming and long queues formed whenever supplies were due. Within a few weeks fresh fish was established in the city as a food for cheap mass consumption and demand continued to grow. Within three years the Leeds and Manchester line was handling some 80 tons of fish a week compared with about 3½ tons before the new arrangements, and a commensurate increase in sources of supply enabled retail prices to be kept low.[6] Such developments prove that demand for fish amongst all classes was there providing the price and quality were right.

The experiment was not restricted to Manchester; from the first the special cheap rates applied to all stations on the lines concerned, and by 1845 a great deal of the fish arriving at Manchester was redistributed to adjacent districts. Supplies were also drawn in from other Yorkshire fishing stations — via the York and North

Midland Railway — as well as from the north east of England. That this venture proved successful owed much to the initiative and endeavour of Captain Laws.

Many places on the Yorkshire coast were not connected directly with the embryonic national railway network until the mid 1840s. In 1845 George Hudson's York and North Midland Railway constructed a line from York to Scarborough, and a spur which left it at Rillington ended the isolation of the Whitby to Pickering line, which was taken over by Hudson's company and converted to steam locomotive traction. The next year Bridlington was reached from Hull and that undertaking was fully extended through Filey to Scarborough by October 1847. The opening of direct rail links to the Yorkshire coast did not make the later 1840s a time of spectacular development for fish trade. Laws' arrangement brought some benefit but in part it merely helped to offset declining trade in other areas such as the export sector. Furthermore, the markets opened up were limited to those towns on the railways which had organised the scheme. Additionally, the Yorkshire coast fishing stations were beginning to face competition from a small but growing Hull trawling industry in the latter half of the decade. However, during the 1850s, as national railway fish carriage policies were hammered out, many other towns and cities were opened up to the trade. By the end of that decade the Yorkshire coast fish salesmen were sending fish by rail to markets as distant as London and Birmingham. Steam trains meant speedier and more reliable deliveries and as a result it was no longer necessary to cure fish heavily for the home market, and lighter cures, such as the kipper and finnon haddock, were developed with an emphasis on taste rather than keeping ability. In short, the railways helped to open the working-class market for fresh and lightly cured fish. To cope with the increased trade there was a massive expansion of the retail sector: between 1841 and 1871 the number of fishmongers enumerated in the census returns more than trebled.[7]

This dramatic restructuring of the distributive and marketing sectors of the fish trade was accompanied by a great expansion of the catching effort: in 1845, 73 first class fishing vessels were registered at the Custom Houses of Whitby, Scarborough and Bridlington, but by 1877 the count was 150 such craft. Taken alone these statistics understate the level of expansion, for by the latter date the average size of fishing vessels was considerably greater and each deployed more gear. The number of fishermen working from the Yorkshire coast almost doubled even though new catching methods and improved boats reduced the number of men needed on each of the larger craft. The growth of the first class fleet was concentrated particularly upon the Scarborough Customs Port area where registrations almost quadrupled. Growth was less evident at Whitby, while the small first class fleet owned by Flamborough fishermen and registered at Bridlington almost disappeared. Nevertheless, almost every fishing community along the coast experienced an increase in catching activity of some sort, if only inshore. However, the most impressive expansion during these decades concerns the development and spread of trawl fishing.

A trawl is a bag-shaped net, attached to the fishing boat by means of strong cables known as warps. It is dragged along the sea bed and traps most of the fish whose path it crosses. These are collected by the force of movement at the 'cod end' of the net. A trawl's catching efficiency is largely determined by the width of its open mouth which, until the 1890s, was kept open by a large beam or length of wood. This is why the gear was known as a 'beam trawl'. The first account of a trawling engine appears in a petition to Edward III in 1376 against its continued usage but until the later eighteenth century trawling was mainly an inshore pursuit centred on Barking and Brixham. An offshore version then spread along the English Channel[8] and up into the Southern Bight of the North Sea towards Yarmouth. During the 1790s forty trawling smacks from Barking found employment on grounds such as the Broad Fourteens and Brown Bent off Yarmouth and some were reported to be operating as far north as Smith's Knoll and apparently almost across the North Sea to Holland.[9] Most accounts also agree that a few craft were exploring the potential of more northerly grounds by the 1830s, and that between 1840 and 1860 trawling spread swiftly along much of the east coast of England and into the central areas of the North Sea. This was the period when Hull and Grimsby established themselves as trawling ports. A further extension included the development of a summer fishing ground between Texel and Terschelling off the Dutch coast. By 1860 trawling was the single most important means of taking white fish from many ports on the east coast of England.

Three factors feature prominently in most explanations of why such a rapid expansion of trawling took place between 1840 and 1860. It is sometimes suggested that the original trawling grounds in the south west may have been denuded of stocks and that this encouraged the migration of smacks. A second stimulant is said to have been the railways, and the third the discovery of the Silver Pits. The first of these, however, can be ruled out swiftly for research has shown that the migration of the Devon smacks to the North Sea around mid century coincided with increased investment in new vessels at ports such as Brixham, which is hardly consistent with the picture of a totally exhausted and declining fishery.[10] With regard to the railways, there certainly does appear to have been a close correlation between their growth and the opening up of the North Sea trawling grounds. But it is not clear why the railways were so vital to the extension of this pursuit since trawling was an ancient, if previously limited, activity. When considering the importance of the Silver Pits to the early trawlermen, it is important to be precise about when large scale exploitation of their resources began and it is also necessary to establish just why these predominantly cold weather grounds should have been so important to the establishment of a permanent — as opposed to a seasonal — trawl fishery from the Yorkshire coast.

A survey of early fishing practices reveals that trawling was by no means new to the area. The Humber shrimp and prawn fishermen deployed gear which consisted of two small trawls that were dragged behind a sailing craft at the turn of the tide. Along the Yorkshire coast itself, fishermen often towed a 'traul' inshore in order to take small fish to bait their great lines, and in Filey Bay manorial rights show that a form of horse-drawn trawl had been in use from the beach for centuries. Further up the coast, at Hartlepool, beam trawling is described in an 1816 account and appears to have been an established method of taking fish inshore. Thus it appears that the basic principles of trawling were understood and even practised in the locality, but prior to the nineteenth century there is no evidence to suggest a widespread commercial application of the method on a scale to rival lining.

The first reference to deeper water trawling for white fish off the Yorkshire coast relates to an experiment carried out by a Flamborough-owned craft, registered at Bridlington, which worked a fishing ground lying south east from Dimlington Heights in south Holderness. This venture met with some success for above 100 pairs of sole were reported as having been taken with one trawl of the net. This experiment appears to have been instigated by Colonel Ralph Creyke of Marton Hall near Flamborough: he was a local magistrate and also treasurer of the Flamborough Fishermen's Fund, a society set up in 1809 with the help of wealthy local individuals as well as subscriptions from fishermen in order to provide benefits in the event of loss of life, boat, gear or infirmity. In the June of 1819 he had registered a 39 foot, 33 ton cutter-rigged craft, the *Moor Park*, which was operated on his behalf by Cornelius Young until the following October. The experiment then was discontinued, but in 1821 Creyke was involved in a Hull Corporation venture in which two Plymouth trawling smacks were induced by financial incentives to try their luck out of the port.[11] That project also met with little immediate success but the seeds of future possibilities may well have been planted in the minds of the visiting south western fishermen.

Ten years later, in 1831, trawling smacks came back, this time to Scarborough. That summer at least two craft were working the local grounds and landing near the harbour. The strangers found a number of attractive features which encouraged them to stay. The town was well established as a fashionable resort of the wealthy and their household entourages, and this seasonal influx greatly swelled the town's population and the demand for provisions. This sharp upturn in demand occurred at precisely the same time as the local fishermen were also busy supplying other outlets both inland and overseas, so that a niche was left in the market which the smackmen were able to exploit and so the practice of seasonal landings was established.

There were, however, occasions when the impact of the trawler landings, through the sheer quantity of fish they netted, tilted the local balance of supply and demand to the disadvantage of the catcher. Such situations fuelled the local men's underlying resentment of the newcomers and occasionally disturbances erupted. In July 1831 local fishermen approached Scarborough magistrates in an attempt to prevent the two west country smacks coming in to sell their fish, but the magistrates informed them that they had no legal right to interfere. The level of dissatisfaction was such that a large number of fishermen took matters into their own hands and gathered on the beach to prevent the two smacks from landing. This action was only partially successful for, although the two boats decided to avoid confrontation by making off, one returned after the crowd had dispersed and landed its catch.[12]

The smackmen must have found their visits profitable for they returned in greater force the following year: towards the end of May 1832 some eight smacks hailing from Ramsgate, Dover and Plymouth arrived in Scarborough harbour, and they evidently intended staying the summer for the crews brought their families along with them. This new invasion rekindled the previous year's animosity and early June was marked by a string of affrays during one of which a southerner was stabbed by a local. Matters became so serious that the local magistrates felt obliged to swear in preventive men as special constables. Following this an uneasy peace returned.[13] The trawlermen continued their visits throughout the 1830s and occasionally there were further outbreaks of unrest. However, the heat was taken out of the situation somewhat as the rest of the decade proved a time of great prosperity for the Yorkshire coast fishermen. It did not take long for this dangerous coastline to claim its first of many trawling victims when the smack *Ann* of Sandwich was wrecked off Scarborough in September 1834.[14] At both Scarborough and Hull — where they also landed — their activities were predominantly seasonal during the 1830s with only a handful of smacks settling permanently at the two ports from the later years of the decade. The first two permanent Scarborough smacks were *Forager* and *Providence*, the former skippered by Thomas Halfyard, a native of Ramsgate, who was later to figure prominently in the development of the Hull fishing industry.[15]

During the 1840s there was a further migration of smacks from the south, largely to Hull which seems to have been more attractive than Scarborough. Indeed, the first two Scarborough-registered smacks also moved to the Humber port in 1842. It has been suggested that Hull was preferred at that time because Scarborough harbour was too small,[16] but its capacity to handle craft was considerably increased from 1844 when the outer harbour, which had previously been almost unusable, was dredged. It seems more likely that the railway arrangement drawn up by Captain Laws made Hull the more attractive initial base and that the absence of any local long-established fishing fleet there meant that the smackmen did not have to contend with the sort of hostility encountered at Scarborough.

All year round trawling was established off the Yorkshire coast during the 1840s (Fig. 3) and more craft arrived each year, but the following decade witnessed a much higher level of migration to both Scarborough and Hull, and then later Grimsby. Within a few years Hull and Grimsby had become the nation's largest white fishing centres. The reason why growth took off from the 1840s is often attributed to the discovery of the Silver Pits but there has been much confusion amongst historians about just when they were first exploited and a range of dates has been put forward between 1837 and 1850. Part of the confusion may well be due to contemporary sources referring to different grounds. The Little Silver Pit is about thirty miles east of Spurn Point, while the Great Silver Pit is further to the north east and closer to the Dogger, and these were just two of the many trawling grounds opened up to trawlers during those years; other rich areas included Botney Gut, Hospital Ground and California. To say that such grounds were discovered by trawlermen is not strictly true. Many were well known to local fishermen, including the ground named by the smackmen as California.[17] What was particularly attractive about grounds such as the Silver Pits were the catches of soles that could be made and it was in this sense that the trawlers discovered the value of the grounds. The local men deployed great lines which did not take many such flat fish. Furthermore, the best sole season in the Silver Pits was in winter when the large local line boats were traditionally laid up in harbour. Thus it was the trawlermen who 'discovered' the sole potential of the grounds.

It has been suggested that the Silver Pits were discovered in 1838, lost, then rediscovered in 1844,[18] a suggestion which would help account for the differing dates put forward. However, it seems unlikely that experienced mariners, once they had located fishing banks and worked them, would fail to find them in future years. It seems possible that their whereabouts were kept secret by the first handful of smack skippers who settled permanently at Hull and Scarborough. It is now clear that large-scale exploitation of the Silver Pits began in the winter of 1844/5. Their value had evidently become common knowledge towards the end of 1844 during a spell of intensely cold weather. The grounds had swiftly attracted the attention of a number of south country smacks which

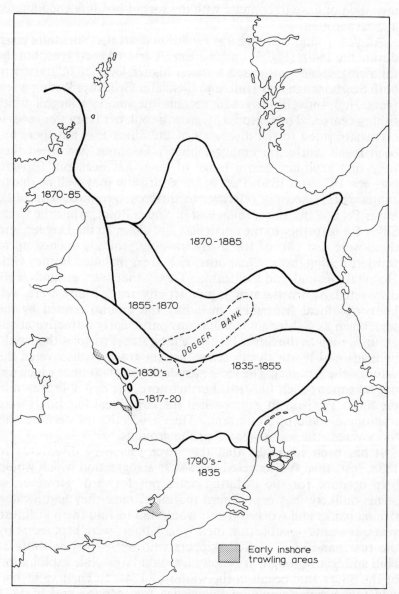

1870-85

1870-1885

1855-1870

DOGGER BANK

1830's

1835-1855

1817-20

1790's -
1835

Early inshore
trawling areas

Figure 3.
Map showing the spread of trawling across the North Sea.

had stayed on after their usual summer season because of the high fish prices prevailing at Hull and Scarborough. The event was recorded in the *Leeds Mercury* because that city, along with several others, benefited almost immediately from the immense numbers of soles that were being forwarded inland.[19] Normally a luxury item, they were retailing at what was regarded as the very low price of 4*d*. to 6*d*. a pair and proved of great benefit to the poor in that time of dearth. The grounds were apparently first known as the Silver Banks and their 'discovery' even warranted a mention in *The Times*.[20] In January 1845 almost double the usual number of smacks were working the grounds off the Dogger Bank and on one day alone some 18,000 pairs of soles were dispatched inland from Hull.[21] In order to cope with the sheer quantities of fish novel methods were devised for getting them to other markets. The bonanza may even have created a forerunner of the later fleeting system, for a number of craft which wished to sell their catch in London packed their fish in hampers, hailed southward bound steamers and transferred their catch to them. This 'discovery' occurred during a time when smack activity out of Hull was increasing thanks to more fishermen settling at the port as well as other crews staying longer than their usual season. However, this sole boom was certainly limited to the cold spells and cannot have sustained the smacks during the rest of the year. Though obviously an attraction, it was largely a bonus and was not the major cause of the migration. This was undoubtedly due to the railways.

A number of factors can be identified which help explain why the railway was so crucial to the establishment of permanent trawling operations off the Yorkshire coast. Most of a smack's typical catch consisted of so-called offal fish, in particular haddock and plaice. These low value fish generally enjoyed only a limited market close to the coast in the pre-railway era because of the high cost of transportation. When the first trawlers visited the coast there was always the danger of glutting the market for such fish so a fair proportion of the offal fish was heaved overboard. Sometimes this meant as much as four-fifths of the catch. Such wasteful modes of operation incurred for trawlermen the wrath of local line fishermen who could usually dispose of most fish they hooked, and it reinforced their belief that trawling was both harmful and destructive of stocks.

The Laws arrangement created a somewhat wider market for offal fish, and this encouraged trawlers to land more of their catch. During the 1850s the market was greatly extended as national rail carriage arrangements conducive to the conveying of offal fish came into operation. Thereafter, trawlers with their large catches of cheap fish were well equipped to cater for the mass market, unlike the great line fishermen who went largely for the quality fish that had previously been the only varieties that could stand transport costs to inland markets. Hull's trawling fleet grew swiftly through the 1850s but on the coast growth was more patchy. The majority of established fishing stations, including Flamborough, Filey, Runswick, Robin Hood's Bay and Staithes, almost completely eschewed the practice. However, at Scarborough the tradition of laying up the first class fleet for the winter was broken from the mid 1840s onwards. Initially, about six yawls were fitted out for trawling after returning from the Yarmouth herring fishery in November, and they were soon joined by others. At Bridlington Quay an inshore version of trawling, which utilised the coble, spread across the Bay.

There was another spate of migration to Scarborough in mid-century. In May 1850 William Toby registered the *Eliza*, a 47 foot one-masted smack, built in Plymouth and previously registered at Hull. In July the *Providence* followed. She was another one-masted smack, also previously registered at Hull, but constructed at Brixham. In October they were joined by the *Zephyr* but she stayed only briefly before moving up the coast. The following year a further five smacks settled. The first, called *Rover*, had been built back at Yarmouth in 1825 and was brought to Scarborough by George Appleyard, a local vessel owner. Another *Rover* was registered which had been built at Cowes in 1793. She was owned by William Alward, a name later to become synonymous with the development of the Grimsby fishing industry. The endeavours of this second wave of settlers proved sufficiently rewarding to attract a further thirteen trawling smacks to the port in the following three years.

There were also attempts to encourage trawling to take root at Whitby, largely promoted by the efforts of local shipowning and commercial interests rather than by south country smackmen who do not seem to have been particularly interested in the port. In 1849 one smack, *King William*, was registered there for a short

50

while but had soon moved back to Exeter. The next arrival's stay was almost equally brief but for a more tragic reason: the *Friends Goodwill* was lost with all hands within a few months of registration. Three further smacks arrived in 1854 but one was soon lost at sea and only two more were registered during the remainder of the decade.[22] By the time the separate fishing vessel register opened in 1869 not one trawler was to be found at Whitby.

The outsider influence in the Scarborough fishing fleet began to wane after 1855. This was largely due to the initiatives being taken at Grimsby by the railway company; in a successful attempt to establish the fishing industry there it offered smackmen from Hull, Scarborough and elsewhere attractive berthing and handling rates and provided lavish facilities. Many vessels were lured to the port, including a number of the smackmen who had arrived at Scarborough in the previous five years. There were other factors involved. George Alward later explained his family's decision to move as being due to the problems of entering Scarborough harbour in winter and the difficulty that the outsiders found in gaining acceptance amongst the local fishing community.[23] The move certainly paid off for his family became one of Grimsby's most prosperous before the turn of the century. After 1855 local men began to figure much more prominently in Scarborough's trawl fishery. Three who stood out were Abraham Appleyard, the local harbour master and shipowner, James Sellers and Henry Wyrill, who was the only working fisherman of the trio. During the 1830s and early 1840s he had been chiefly employed on merchant vessels in the Baltic trade, but by 1845 he was part owner of a two-masted yawl.[24] Hard work and determination paid off for by 1859 he had interests in at least four trawling smacks, although it seems unlikely that he still went to sea regularly for he had become well established as both smackowner and fish salesman. The last-named occupation was to prove particularly remunerative during the 1850s and 1860s. Individuals engaged in that branch of the business gained in prosperity thanks to the ever-growing volume of fish sales which passed through their hands as the railways widened and extended the national market. Such wealth induced them to invest in the catching sector and none proved more successful than James Sellers. He was born at Malton in 1820 and until 1845 was engaged with his father in the fish traffic from the coast to that town. After the opening of the railway he moved to Scarborough and, like Wyrill, began to develop commercial connections with inland towns for the forwarding and sale of sea fish. In 1852 he acquired a Brixham-built smack, *Happy Return*, and was soon on his way to building up a substantial holding in the fleet.

Both Sellers and Wyrill differed from the traditional Yorkshire coast fishing vessel owners in that they were not only willing to promote trawling but were also prepared to acquire craft with the aid of mortgages. Traditionally, an individual who could not afford to purchase a vessel outright took on partners, but by arranging a mortgage a craft could be acquired without entering such partnerships. James Sellers used mortgages to build up a fleet of vessels which helped establish him as the largest fishing vessel owner on the Yorkshire coast. Yet neither he, nor Wyrill nor Appleyard, limited themselves to that system. They also bought their way into other craft by acquiring half or quarter shares and soon had interests in the line and herring fisheries as well.[25]

The 1850s and 1860s were also notable for a change in the way the Yorkshire coast's traditional first class fishing fleet was rigged. The lug rig had remained usual for line fishing vessels; it made for swift sailing but its disadvantages became apparent when the first few craft tried trawling, for it proved unwieldy when towing and required a large crew to operate. Thus it eventually gave way to a form of gaff rig which provided the manoeuvrability important when trawling and allowed a smaller crew to be carried. One disadvantage — which was to prove crucial later — was that it knocked a knot or two off a craft's top speed. By the end of the 1860s the new rig was to be found on most traditional types of first class fishing craft, although they were still described as yawls. As great lining catches declined, the gaff rig was even adopted at non-trawling stations, for it meant that smaller crews were needed.

Scarborough remained the only fishing station with a first class trawling fleet during these decades, although during the later 1850s the number of specialist trawling smacks declined as many of those who had settled during the earlier 1850s were lured to Grimsby. However, trawling as a whole did not decline at Scarborough, for there was an increasing use of gaff rigged yawls as trawlers outside the herring season. Many vessels adopted not a dual but a triple role; their seasonal round of activity included a herring season during the summer, and an alternation between trawling and lining over the remainder of the year.

There were few trawlers on the Yorkshire coast apart from those at Scarborough and Bridlington. Both Filey and Staithes possessed healthy fleets of first class fishing vessels, but neither exhibited any inclination to try their hand at trawling. This attitude was typified by a Flamborough witness to the 1863-6 Royal Commission on the British Fisheries: when asked why local men did not try trawling when line fishing would not pay, he replied:

> We were brought up to hook and line fishing and we cannot think of commencing anything else. We never did anything at this place but fish with a hook and line and follow the herring fishing and the mackerel fishing a little.[26]

Stations such as Flamborough were perhaps too small for direct operations by first class fishing vessels but were suitable for adopting an inshore variant, as twentieth-century events were to prove. The few individuals who did try trawling at Filey and Whitby were very much exceptions to the rule. One important reason was the strength of tradition among the local communities and their hostility to trawling; they were close-knit, inter-related societies where individuals relied closely upon each other in the course of their day-to-day activities. Few outsiders joined them as the same families tended to dominate each community throughout the nineteenth century. Yet another factor was economic; in general, linesmen benefited during the fifties and sixties from the expansion of marketing opportunities, which reduced any incentive to alter their usual seasonal round of operations.

During the 1860s another batch of specialist trawling smacks was registered at Scarborough but this time by owners such as Sellers and Wyrill. Many more dual purpose vessels were also acquired. New yawls were usually turned out by builders in Scarborough and Whitby, but many of the trawling smacks acquired were second-hand and sometimes of considerable age. When new smacks were ordered, their buyers at first preferred to go further afield and have them constructed at more traditional smack-building centres in the south. In the 1870s, however, with markets continuing to expand and prices holding, the industry enjoyed something of an investment boom. More capital than ever was ventured in the construction of trawling smacks, especially by Messrs Sellers and Wyrill and for the first time boat builders at Scarborough began to take a lead in such construction. The first two trawling smacks to be built locally had been turned out in 1867/8[27] but during the 1870s the majority were from Yorkshire coast yards. This was valuable business and enabled the remnants of the local shipbuilding industry to survive at Scarborough when orders for other vessels were dwindling.

There was also a gradual increase in the size of new smacks which enabled them to carry ever larger beam trawls, thus increasing their catching capacity. When details of Scarborough smacks registered between 1850 and 1854 are analysed it can be seen that their length varied between 36 and 56 feet; by the 1870s newly registered sailing smacks ranged in size from 62 to 80 feet, with the bulk of new craft exceeding 70 feet. Trawls then incorporated a beam up to 48 feet wide compared with 38 feet which had been usual in the 1840s. The traditional rope warps were replaced by ones of steel and gradually steam capstans were fitted to the smacks which proved much more efficient than the old man-powered capstans. Such developments made it possible to work deeper water grounds and thus open up much more of the North Sea. Additionally, some of the older smacks were lengthened to enable them to carry larger beam trawls. This in itself was an interesting process. The craft was not docked but dealt with on the open beach within Scarborough harbour. Everything moveable was stripped out, including masts, spars and ballast. The smack was then 'neaped', that is, hauled as far out of the water as possible on a spring tide. It was then cut through at the greatest beam and pulled apart by block and tackle. A new piece of keel was fitted between the sections, the space above built up, and the boat was soon ready for refloating.[28]

The increasing size of both boats and gear was inevitably accompanied by a rise in costs. In the early 1860s a trawling smack straight off the stocks and fully fitted out would usually cost between £700 and £900, through occasionally up to £1000. By the 1880s a new vessel of the latest design cost in the region of £1500. The price of gear rose similarly and such factors gradually made it more difficult for the working fisherman to acquire his own vessel. The fleet at Scarborough therefore fell increasingly into the hands of those smackowners and fish merchants who held the most substantial financial resources.

In terms of fish landed, Scarborough was not outstripped as a fishing port by Hull and Grimsby until the early 1860s, although

54

those two stations had been catching more white fish by the end of the previous decade. Yet in the mid 1870s Scarborough was still well established as the most northerly of the North Sea trawling stations, boasting a fleet of some forty specialist smacks and at least fifty more dual-purpose vessels which crowded all parts of the harbour to absolute capacity. Trawling was then the principal mode of capture employed by vessels registered at the port and such operations were coming increasingly under the control of a small group of wealthy self-made individuals of whom James Sellers and Henry Wyrill were the most prominent. The industry was enjoying a period of rapid growth and the catching sector was spreading its nets ever further afield. Not only did Scarborough trawlers join the boxing fleets sailing out of Hull and Grimsby but they also ranged across the North Sea to the coasts of Holland and Denmark. This practice — so universally abhorred some thirty-five or so years earlier — had become part and parcel of the port's fishing tradition.

VI

The Herring, Line and Inshore Fisheries 1840-1879

For the British herring fisheries as a whole, the 1840s were to prove a decade of mixed fortune. In Scotland, the main centre of the industry at that time, high prices were prevalent over the years 1835-42 but within a few seasons the trade was afflicted by a depression in activity. The decline of the West Indian market for pickle cured herrings in the later thirties, after the emancipation of the slaves to whom they had been fed by the plantation owners, gave a hint of what was to come but had not in itself caused a slump in trade. This was brought about when Irish demand first faltered and then collapsed in the wake of the 1845 Potato Famine. Though the Continent was an important and growing market, demand from that source was then not strong enough to compensate for this reverse. However, its continued growth after mid-century was to revive prosperity north of the border and usher in an almost unbroken era of expansion that lasted until 1884.[1]

In contrast, the Yorkshire coast herring fishery did not rely heavily on such overseas markets and by the 1840s was selling mainly to the rest of England. Exploitation of the shoals increased cautiously over the decade. The years 1840-42 were marked by good catches and prosperity with local interest reaching a new height in 1842 as the low prices being offered for dried cod induced many vessels to abandon the great line fishery and embark upon the quest for herring much earlier in the year than was usual.[2] The 1843 season proved to be poor, though this seems to have been due to local difficulties in locating the shoals rather than any diminution in home demand. Some degree of forward momentum was lost over the remainder of the decade as the first class fishing fleet shrank in size. Overall growth was on a more sluggish scale than had been the case in the thirties, but at least it continued.

Three main factors combined to allow this limited expansion to be sustained on the Yorkshire coast. First, the reduction in the strength of the first class fishing fleet was largely due to a decline in dry curing activities and the problems facing the great line fishery as a whole, but many of the yawls and luggers that remained in service spent more of their time in pursuit of herrings than ever before. Furthermore, at that time large decked vessels were of less importance in the catching of herrings for many shoals were located on the 'inside' as well as the 'outside' grounds. Whereas the last named were often well over thirty miles from the coast and called for the employment of large sea-going decked vessels, the former were within fourteen miles of the coast and often in the range of smaller undecked craft whose numbers were on the increase over the decade.[3]

Secondly, the catching effort deployed by each boat increased over the decade. Many specialist inshore herring craft were constructed and could carry more nets than the cobles they displaced without needing a larger crew. The first class vessels also carried more nets for from 1842 the practice spread amongst the five-man boat fleet of discarding the main mast. At first this was for the duration of the herring fishery but later it became permanent. Though it has been suggested that this step was taken because smuggling, and therefore the need to be speedy if chased by the Revenue vessels, was on the decline,[4] it is more likely to have occurred because the absence of the main mast allowed more nets to be carried and used. However, all craft could carry more nets in a given space as cotton nets began to replace the traditional hemp nets which were heavier and more bulky. The cotton nets were at first supplied by a Musselborough manufacturer who successfully mechanised their production, whereas the old hemp ones had been the product of domestic labour in each fishing community. The combined result was a dramatic increase in catching effort per vessel. Prior to the 1840s Yorkshire coast first class craft had deployed a maximum of 50 or 60 nets each but by mid-century they were carrying up to 90; this increase continued and by 1863 the largest yawls could shoot between 120 and 130 nets apiece.

The third factor was the most important: overland demand

increased following the Laws railway arrangement and, had it not been limited to such a few companies, it seems likely that the expansion of the Yorkshire herring trade would have been much brisker during the 1840s.

After the introduction of national railway fish carriage agreements in the following decade, landings and demand increased markedly. The railways helped to shift the entire emphasis of the English herring trade from the export sector to the home market. Unlike many of the Scottish fisheries, they were well placed to exploit the growing internal demand for provisions. Faster transport meant that milder and less thoroughly cured products could be sold. These were cured for taste and thus often more attractive to the English consumer than traditional cures such as the red herring. Two mildly cured products which rose to national prominence over the following decades were the Yarmouth bloater and the Newcastle kipper.

Increased demand in the later 1850s, after the introduction of cheaper national rail rates, prompted a major expansion in landings on the Yorkshire coast and the resultant prosperity encouraged a new spate of yawl building so that more 'outside' grounds could be worked. In the first half of the decade only two of these craft were built and registered at Scarborough Custom House, whereas in the second half some thirty-four new vessels of this type were registered and based at either Scarborough or Filey. No such new craft had been registered at Whitby during 1850-4 but some thirteen were added in the following five years, and they were based largely on Staithes, a community still without direct rail access. To overcome this disadvantage its fish were dispatched by cart to Goathland station each working day. Such was the demand for new yawls that the local boatbuilders were stretched to their utmost:[5] the majority were turned out in Scarborough and Whitby yards but the demand was sometimes so great that prospective buyers went to Yarmouth and Hull with their orders.

The three fishing communities which benefited most directly from this prosperity were Scarborough, Whitby and, to a lesser extent, Staithes. They were the main landing points for boats from other parts of the country, as well as for craft from Filey, Flamborough, Redcar and other local fishing stations. Their attraction to fishermen was due largely to the presence of herring merchants who used those places as bases during the season.

Where competition amongst buyers was at its greatest the fishermen expected to get the best prices for their catch. As many as 300 to 400 strangers might be found at Staithes during the herring season as early as the mid-1840s[6] and in spite of the growing importance of the home market their number included visiting buyers from Holland and France. Yarmouth merchants were also strongly in evidence at all three landing points. The upsurge in trade was reflected in the levels of rail traffic. In 1857 Whitby shipped out some 350 tons of fish by rail in three days at the height of the season, requiring the use of some 130 wagons. Considerable quantities also left the port by boat.[7] In order to keep pace with the increased landings at Scarborough modest improvements were made to the West Pier in 1860 but these were considered insufficient by the fish trade which continued to press the harbour commissioners for a major reconstruction programme. At Whitby a new fish quay some 750 feet long was constructed in the same year just above the bridge chiefly for the use of the herring trade. Both Scarborough and Whitby continued to attract more and more visiting craft during the 1850s and 1860s. As early as 1852 the number of boats from other parts of the coast that visited Scarborough almost equalled home port vessels: most came from Cley, Cromer and Yarmouth, but by the opening of the next decade many of the seasonal arrivals were voyaging from as far away as St Ives and Penzance.

In spite of the greater levels of exploitation, markets were rarely glutted for more than a day or so. Price levels remained attractive and some remarkable profits were made. The most prosperous years were probably 1856 and 1857; one newly-constructed yawl, the *Olive Branch* of Scarborough, earned an average of £1,100 over both herring seasons.[8] In earlier decades a good return from a full year's fishing would have been unlikely to have approached that figure. The 1860s were mostly prosperous and the trade was by then sufficiently robust to overcome a major setback: on 9 June 1860, thirteen of Filey's fleet of twenty-two yawls were lost in a great gale that caused damage and shipwreck up and down the coast. Ten were swept from their moorings and dashed against the rocks at Speeton. One vessel, the *Sarah*, was carried round Flamborough Head and picked up by a craft twenty miles beyond before being towed into Grimsby little the worse for the experience. Several fishermen put off from the shore in spite of

59

the ferocity of the sea in attempts to secure the vessels and one lost his life. The property loss was estimated at upwards of £10,000 and it was rumoured that half the town was bankrupt,[9] yet all losses were made good within three years even though many of the craft had not been insured.[10] Such was the return to be expected from the herring fishery. Indeed, by that time the Yorkshire herring fishery was amongst the most profitable around the coasts of Britain. The prospect of a successful voyage was sufficient to entice a number of Scottish vessels to Scarborough and Whitby when their home seasons were still in full swing. For much of the 1850s and early 1860s the quality of the fish landed was high and the length of time that shoals were to be found in abundance off the coast was longer than was considered normal either before or after. Previously the season had begun in late July or early August but by 1851 it often opened in early June and lasted until late November. This caused the fishermen to end their usual practice of repairing to the East Anglian herring fishery in the autumn as they had done for at least 200 years. By the late 1850s the Yorkshire coast herring fishery was lasting almost five months and was considered to be more remunerative at many fishing stations than all other branches of the industry put together.

The relative strengths of the visiting herring fleets changed with the passing of the season: in 1862, one of the last of the really long seasons, landings at Whitby were dominated during the months of June and July by vessels from Buckhaven on the Fifeshire coast; during August most catches were landed by St Ives, Penzance and Scarborough craft. The Cornish boats had often previously engaged in herring fisheries off the Isle of Man and Ireland and they usually departed before the middle of October to take advantage of their home fishery. Few East Anglian vessels were landing at Whitby by the early 1860s for they seem to have preferred Scarborough. The last months of the season at both ports were left largely to the Yorkshire coast vessels.

As the 1860s wore on, the herring shoals lived up to their reputation for unpredictability and catches during the early months shrank to negligible levels although seasonal landings continued on an upward, though fluctuating, trend. Although shoaling for a shorter period they were fished with an ever greater intensity; by 1863/4 not less than a hundred boats were entering Scarborough harbour at the peak of each season and up to 300 more were discharging their catches into small boats while moored outside.[11] About twice as many men were employed in this fishery than twenty years earlier.

Landings were made by both the larger decked vessels that worked on the 'outside' grounds and by the open boats which fished closer to land. During the 1870s the yield from the open boat fishery began to fall off especially in the south of the county. Whether this was due to overfishing is open to doubt for it may well have been a further manifestation of the herring's unpredictable habits. The off-shore grounds continued to be profitable while the inshore fishermen found drifting less remunerative than in earlier decades.

The prosperity of the herring fishery continued to make both Scarborough and Whitby a magnet for visiting merchants. Only two or three resided permanently at Whitby but during the summer months upwards of twenty-eight might be found there. Scarborough possessed about eight permanent merchants but their ranks were also swelled greatly during the summer. The majority still came from East Anglia and B.M. Bradbeer seems to have been one of the most important. His home base was Lowestoft but he was a regular visitor from the late 1850s to the 1880s. Come September he would usually have operations underway at both Scarborough and Whitby. Few such men settled permanently but one concern that became established belonged to the Woodger family. Although originating in North Sunderland this family had, by way of Newcastle, made Lowestoft its main base. In the later 1850s Frederick Woodger opened operations at Scarborough and a couple of decades later these were being managed by Henry Lamble Woodger. Initially interested in smoke curing — and this family is credited with inventing the kipper — they soon diversified and by the end of the 1870s were involved in all aspects of the port's fishing industry.[12] Messrs Sellers and Wyrill also developed a keen interest in the herring fishery over these decades.

Exploitation of the herring shoals continued to intensify into the 1870s. During the 1870 season some hundred wagons were needed to move 300 tons of herring out of Whitby on one Tuesday in September.[13] Scarborough was perhaps even more prosperous and attracted a greater number of vessels because the port's harbour commissioners had bought a steam tug which provided a valuable service towing the sail-powered fishing boats to and from the grounds at times of adverse or light winds. The years following 1876 were particularly prosperous with a continual increase in the numbers of vessels participating in the fishery and larger landings were noted than ever before. The latest additions to the fleet of Yorkshire yawls were of the largest dimensions hitherto built and were considerably bigger vessels than those constructed in earlier decades. This prosperity was based on a buoyant demand for herring which meant that prices remained high even though the weight of fish landed on the quayside was of record proportions.

By the 1870s the proportion of the local herring catch destined for overseas markets was negligible.[14] Most were sold on a home market which extended from London, across midland cities such as Birmingham, through Lancashire and into the north east. A fair amount was consumed fresh, but lightly smoked varieties enjoyed a growing demand and the name 'kipper' had come into common use. Thus in the herring fishery there were considerable developments and some important changes initially stimulated by the advent of improved and cheaper transportation. As with the trawl fishery, the creation of a relatively large market by the railways stimulated a rapid expansion of catching effort along the Yorkshire coast.

The experience of the line fisheries from the 1840s differed somewhat from that of other branches of the local trade. That decade was the last during which the Fishery Commissioners in Edinburgh monitored the performance of fisheries in England, but their surviving records give some idea of the changes that were taking place in the Yorkshire line fisheries. At the close of the 1830s long-established custom and practice still held sway. The fleet of large luggers, supplemented by the newer yawls, working on the rich cod grounds off the Dogger Bank, constituted the most important branch of white fishing in the area. The two main fishing stations were still Staithes and Filey, in spite of developments at Scarborough. The most important outlets were equally traditional, being either the tables of the wealthy inland English, or the London and Spanish markets. But this was almost the end of an era. Within a decade great changes occurred as a result of which dry curing and the export trade were reduced to an insignificant level. Furthermore, though all types of lining were to remain important and even flourishing pursuits, such operations were to decline in relative importance as trawl fishing gained momentum.

By 1839 the increasing quantity of quality cured fish coming out of the Shetlands was causing prices to fall and the depression this caused for the Yorkshire trade continued into the following year leading to a cut in production by the local curers. But prices revived in 1841 with good demand coming largely from London which still preferred the Yorkshire product. During that year some local curers, anxious to take advantage of prices which reached £22 per ton, presented their fish to the Fishery Commissioners' officer before it was thoroughly dried and thus failed to secure the official punch of approval and the best return. Nevertheless, relative prosperity stimulated a revival of interest in 1842 and a greater output;[15] the amount cured would have been still greater had not the latter end of the season been afflicted once more by low prices which encouraged the fishermen and curers to turn to the herring fishery much earlier than usual. That year proved to be the last one in which dry curing activities were pursued with anything like their old vigour along the Yorkshire coast and production rapidly fell away. For many of those involved in the trade the herring fishery came to be the most profitable summer activity, though many craft found it increasingly worthwhile to land catches at sea ports along the coasts of Durham and Northumberland, while the railway trade through Hull also grew in importance.[16] Gradually, the various communities ran down their dry curing operations. They were given over at Flamborough in 1844 and Scarborough harbour records show that no rents were collected for drying fish on the piers after 1842. Within a few years commercial production had all but ceased and only Staithes persevered with the practice as late as 1863; even there production was by then running at less than ten per cent of its former level.[17] Thus old curing techniques fell into disuse and were forgotten. When English dry curing was revived at the end of the nineteenth century in order to satisfy Mediterranean demand it was nurtured by the 'new' fishing ports of Hull and Grimsby rather than by the old centres along the Yorkshire coast.

Over the same years alterations were made to line fishing practice. Smaller crews were shipped and it became usual for the larger craft to carry just one coble to sea on their decks instead of two. To compensate, the length of the great line and the number of hooks deployed per crew member was gradually increased, but contemporary reports suggest that the yield per fisherman was on the decline. However, the system seems to have been buoyed up by the higher prices that many varieties of fish were fetching on the quayside as the railways revolutionised the nature and scope of the inland market.

Seasonal practices also changed. Concentration on the herring fishery meant that great lining virtually ceased during the months of June to August, although many vessels fitted out for drifting carried a few hand lines to sea for taking cod. The length and prosperity of the herring season also determined whether the large boats returned to great lining for the final months of the year before being laid up for the winter, although the break was being shortened by the 1860s and the Staithes fleet was sometimes in operation by the middle of February. Though the economic incentives to lengthen the yawl's working season — and thus increase the return — were considerable, so were the accompanying risks. Bad weather was prevalent during the winter months and local harbours remained notoriously difficult to enter in such conditions. The onset of an unexpected storm could scatter the fleet along the length of the coast. The earlier in the year the vessels fitted out the more likely were such incidents to occur; in February 1865 sixteen of the Staithes yawls were caught on the fishing grounds by a violent storm. It was several days before the local press learned that six of the craft had managed to make Hartlepool, that three others had sought shelter in Bridlington Bay, and a further two in Runswick Bay: one vessel was known to have been wrecked and the other three were not heard of for several more days.[18] The disruption and anguish felt by the community was considerable and such incidents served as grim reminders of why the winter lay-up was part and parcel of traditional fishing practice.

The zenith of great lining vessel design was probably reached in 1862 with the launch of the lugger *Contrast*. Built by Samuelson of Hull for Josiah Hudson, a Scarborough shipowner, the craft incorporated traditional and modern maritime practice: a three-masted lugger, she was, at 65 feet, longer than her predecessors and was the first Yorkshire coast fishing vessel to be constructed with an iron hull.[19] Hudson aimed to expand the great line fishery for *Contrast* was intended not only to work on the North Sea grounds but also on the reputedly rich cod banks off Rockall.

During the 1870s the number of craft that followed the great line fishery declined. A principal reason was the difficulty of obtaining regular and cheap supplies of bait. When trawlers had first arrived they provided an additional source of bait, thanks to their large catches of offal fish, but by the 1870s a great deal of it could be sold for human consumption. One alternative was to purchase barrels of Scottish and East Anglian herrings but they were also rising in price and this cut into profit margins. Moreover, supplies were often disrupted and there were frequent complaints about craft being unable to put to sea through a lack of bait. To add to all this the line fishermen found that catches were falling away. The response at Scarborough was that more yawls than ever turned from lining to trawling outside the herring season. Even the *Contrast* abandoned great lining and was converted into a trawling smack. By that decade fishermen at Flamborough, Runswick and Robin Hood's Bay had all but lost their interest in the larger luggers and worked mainly from open boats. Even so, Filey and Staithes continued to reject trawling and steadfastly maintained lining with their large fleets of yawls.

The inshore fisheries also benefited from the expansion of the herring fishery and the growth in marketing opportunities. Many inshore fishing communities experienced a marked expansion of activity over the fifty or so years after 1815, especially after 1840: the number of cobles licensed at Flamborough by 1817 was 49 but during 1869 the same community placed 169 inshore fishing craft on the newly opened fishing vessel register; Bridlington Quay possessed only 16 licensed cobles in 1817, and most of those only fished on a part-time basis, but by the end of 1869 there were 49 fishing cobles and mules. Even more remarkable was the growth of the Whitby inshore fishing industry: in early 1818 there were just 13 cobles licensed for fishing, but by 1869 the fleet had grown to 123. Growth also occurred at Staithes, Scarborough and Filey. The fishing communities of Runswick and Robin Hood's Bay were exceptions and both suffered a long-term decline in the strength of their inshore fleets as many of their fishing families seem to have been lured to Whitby with its conveniently-situated railway station.[20]

The prosperity connected with this growth was tempered to some extent by a fall off in the average size of landings. Although nineteenth-century fishermen were notorious for crying wolf there is some justification to back up the inshore men's complaints. Along the whole of the Yorkshire coast and much further north

65

they complained consistently that catches had fallen off. When questioned on this matter by the 1863-6 Royal Commission on the Sea Fisheries, all pinpointed the decline to the introduction of first class trawling in the 1840s and claimed that this had confined them to a far smaller area of the sea bed because of the danger of damage to their gear when trawl nets passed over it. They had retreated to the rocky grounds on which the trawlermen could not operate for fear of fouling their nets. Such blatant disregard for the operations of the linemen had been shown by some trawlermen that the former had been forced off grounds they had worked for generations. One such ground which was abandoned by Flamborough line fishermen in the 1840s was that named California by the trawlermen who 'discovered' it.[21] Although catches fell the smaller landings fetched more money than larger ones had done in the pre-railway era. Moreover, the inshore men's income was also greatly enhanced by the herring fishery, which many regarded as the most profitable and important part of their seasonal round of activity.

Although most inshore fishermen remained hostile to trawling it did take root at Bridlington Quay, which became the most important inshore trawling centre on the Yorkshire coast. Two factors encouraged its establishment there: the bay offered a considerable area of soft-bottomed sea-bed ideal for trawling, and there was no really strong fishing community already existing in the town, so that those who wished to trawl did not have to contend with the hostility of their fellow fishermen. Some of those who took up trawling came from other coastal towns and villages, but many were locals who had previously been engaged in servicing the passing collier fleets. Such fleets had been thinning in number since the construction of the railways and trawling provided an obvious alternative way of earning an income. Others who joined had wider maritime experience and were described in 1863 as a 'race of men . . . who have served perhaps seven years to the sea and then get up one of those boats (cobles) and go trawling'.[22] Such cobles, usually crewed by just two men, were rigged with a fore lug and jib, and pulled a trawl with a beam of between 20 and 24 feet. Their trawling season usually lasted from about February to October with line fishing in the other months, and by 1869 forty-two Bridlington Quay cobles were trawling.

Another inshore activity that benefited from the growth of

marketing opportunities was the crab and lobster fishery. In earlier times exploitation of the Yorkshire coast shell fisheries had been quite limited and the few craft involved were usually crewed by old men and youngsters afloat for the first time. Most shell fish were retailed locally although some were dispatched to places such as York in containers placed on the tops of stage-coaches. As with white fish it had proved economical to send only those of the highest quality any distance and their carriage was complicated by the need to ensure that those dispatched alive survived the journey. The method of capture then employed by Yorkshire fishermen reflected the constraints of the market. Prior to mid-century almost all were taken with 'trunks', or rings as they were sometimes called. The trunk consisted of an iron hoop about five feet in diameter from which was attached a basket-like net of about three feet in depth, and the bait, usually plaice or dabs, was fastened to the hoop by a band stretched across the centre and the whole device was then lowered to the sea bed. When it was properly set the ring and net lay flat on the ground and the idea was to attract, by means of the bait, crabs and lobsters into the middle of the hoop. As there was nothing to then prevent them leaving the bait while it lay on the sea bed it was necessary to examine each trunk frequently. Great skill and much caution were required when hauling one up for if the fish took alarm it might still escape over the top of the device. The trunk was designed to take only the largest and most valuable shell fish as the mesh of the net was large enough to let the smaller ones escape as it was being hauled up. Each trunk was marked on the surface by a cork buoy and a line of them, seldom more than twenty-four, had larger floats placed at each end. This method of capture had several disadvantages. In the first place, it was essential that the fishermen remain constantly with their gear in order to take any shell fish on the bait. As trunking was carried on after dusk, much of the night might be spent by these traps since each trunk had to be checked every 30 to 40 minutes otherwise the crab or lobster could have eaten the bait and moved on. Because of such regular attention, few crews could deal effectively with more than a score of trunks and another drawback was that trunking could only be carried on successfully in water less than 10 fathoms deep, so a number of grounds further out remained unexploited. Yet for all its relative inefficiency, trunking did provide a few fishermen with the type of crabs and lobsters that yielded the best return and posed no dangers of exhausting the stocks.[23]

After the coming of the railways the market for crabs and lobsters was gradually extended to cover much of the country: by 1876 Whitby crabs were being sent to Darlington, Manchester, Liverpool, Leeds and other such places, while Birmingham was supplied by Scarborough. The reduced costs of travel meant that smaller crabs and lobsters were worth landing for they too could find a ready market inland. It is, therefore, not surprising that the inshore fishermen began to adopt an improved method of capture found in some other areas: this was the creel or pot. The creel, still in common use today, is less discriminating about the size of the fish it can take but this was of far less importance after the 1840s. It has two funnel-shaped entrances through which the crab and lobster must pass to take the bait. Unfortunately for the shell fish, the route back is virtually impossible to take. This type of trap has several advantages over the trunk: although a degree of expertise is needed when placing the creels, no real skill is required for the actual process of capture; creels did not need constant attention and once they had laid their pots the fishermen could return to shore until it was time to check them; relieved of the need to make constant checks each crew could work more traps; finally, creels could also be laid in deeper water than trunks and this increased the area of the sea bed that could be exploited. Creels were introduced on to the Yorkshire coast about mid-century and within about ten years most crabs and lobsters were being taken with them. By 1863 the only community which stuck to the trunk was Flamborough whose fishermen were proud of their skills; they appeared to be contemptuous of those who fished with the creel and one of their number told the 1863 Royal Commission on Sea Fisheries that 'any tailor or landsmen could lay them.'[24] Nevertheless, even this prejudice was soon overcome for an 1876 survey reported that trunking was all but extinct along the Yorkshire coast. One result of this changeover was a marked increase in the catching power of each coble and the continually expanding market encouraged more crews to join this fishery. At Scarborough the fleet of cobles going crabbing rose from half a dozen in the 1820s to almost forty in the 1870s, and this story was repeated up and down the coast.

The trunks which creamed off only the highest quality crabs and lobsters posed no real threat to stocks, yet after mid-century the season often lasted from March to October and the larger fleets were deploying up to sixty creels per boat compared with the former maximum of twenty-four trunks. Not surprisingly there were soon complaints about falling catches off the Yorkshire coast and elsewhere which prompted the setting up of a Royal Commission in 1876. Its report found that along the Yorkshire coast from Filey Brigg northwards there had been a gradual and serious decline in the yield of large crabs and lobsters per boat, even though more traps were set. It noted that the railways had created a demand for even the small crabs and lobsters and these were now landed without being allowed to reach maturity and breed. In response, Parliament passed an Act prohibiting the landing of immature crabs measuring less than four and a half inches across the back.

Taken as a whole the 1860s probably witnessed the zenith of the Yorkshire coast inshore fisheries and it is doubtful if they have supported a larger labour force or more boats either before or since. Apart from the problems already discussed there was another growing problem which made itself felt increasingly in the 1870s: supplies of bait were causing concern. The great increase in line fishing activity from inshore vessels, as well as the spread of creels, meant a greatly increased demand for bait. Traditionally, shell fish bait such as cockles and mussels had been collected by women and young children along the shoreline, while some communities, such as Flamborough, dredged up shell fish from the sea bed. By the later 1850s local supplies were totally inadequate and the Yorkshire inshore fisheries were increasingly reliant on distant sources, but alternative sources of supply in the Wash and Tees were also having to cope with increasing demand from other areas. Moreover, the arrival of the railways increased the human consumption of Wash cockles and mussels and large quantities were forwarded to the Midlands. Agriculture also made its demands and there were several complaints about farmers taking cart loads of shell fish to spread as manure on their fields.

That the beds were being depleted was evident to contemporaries and it was clear that they would not recover without some policy of conservation. Yet attempts to introduce a licensing and control system for the Tees beds foundered on the opposition of the local fishermen it was designed to protect. Though content to see others restricted they did not wish their own activities to be curtailed or to be made to pay a licence fee. The whole scheme had to be abandoned in 1860 after it was upheld that they had an un-fettered right under a charter granted by Elizabeth I to collect mussels from the beds. In the Wash, conservation measures were not introduced until 1870 but gales and sharp frosts over the ensuing decade further depleted the remaining stocks. Not un-naturally, this fall off in supplies of shell fish was a factor of critical importance. Bait prices rose steeply and the fishermen even had to look to the Continent, in particular Hamburg, for shell fish. By the later 1870s a bushel of mussels might cost in the region of 2s. 6d. compared with about 10d. in the early 1860s, making a coble's annual bait bill rise from about £20 to £60. Moreover, supplies became less reliable and boats often failed to put to sea for lack of bait. The bait problem therefore had a marked effect on the viability of inshore line fishing and it is perhaps not surprising that the practice was being pursued less vigorously by the late 1870s.[25]

Once more, it is clear that the railways played a major part in encouraging change. To a certain degree, however, the buoyant conditions they created carried with them the seeds for the potential destruction of this same prosperity. The overall response to the increased market demand was to fish more intensively, but this placed greater strain on stocks and the inshore fisheries were soon depleting their resources and paying the price for the absence of any agreed codes of operational practice and conservation. However, during the 1870s the inshore decline was only marginal and overall the decades from 1840 to 1880 were remarkable for evidence of both growth and changes in traditional practice.

VII

The Establishment of Steam Fishing 1877-1914

The transition from sail to steam began amongst the English white fishing fleet. Progress, once successfully underway, was rapid. In 1876 there were no commercial steam fishing vessels in operation but over the following five years a large number of paddle tugs were adapted for fishing and soon afterwards purpose-built steam trawlers began to appear. By the close of the 1880s ports such as Hull and Grimsby had already embarked upon the rapid replacement of their sailing smacks by steam trawlers, while the emergent trawling centres of North Shields and Aberdeen based their expansion almost wholly on steam power. In 1900 Hull became the first English port to completely dispense with white fish sailing vessels. The herring fishery was somewhat slower in following suit. The first commercially viable English steam drifter did not come off the stocks until 1897,[1] but within a few years a large proportion of the Scottish and East Anglian fleets were steam powered. One traditional criticism levelled at the Victorian fishing industry is that it was slow to avail itself of the benefits of steam power,[2] but recent research would suggest that the importance of steam power in the emergence of industrial Britain has been overstressed.[3] Many areas of the economy continued, for rational economic reasons, to remain reliant upon more traditional sources of power, such as wind and water, until well into the second half of the nineteenth century. Nor can it be argued that steam powered fishing was not introduced at an earlier date because of any innate conservatism in the industry. Although there were some communities reluctant to embrace change, there were others, including Hull, Grimsby and Scarborough, that contained

71

progressive elements prepared to adapt and exploit any number of successful innovations: the spread of beam trawling, the introduction of ice, the constant improvement of the wind powered sailing vessel and the development of lighter cured consumer products bear eloquent testimony. Moreover, attempts to apply the steam engine to the exploitation of the fishing grounds predate the last quarter of the nineteenth century.

Maritime steam power had been proved a commercial proposition during the three decades that followed the introduction of steam boats on the Clyde in 1812 and the Humber about 1814. By the 1850s steam fishing experiments were being carried out; in 1853 a steamer was constructed for the Deep Sea Fishing Association of Scotland and in Grimsby two steam fishing vessels were put into service in 1856. None of these ventures met with any long-term success and the Grimsby vessels had their engines removed after being unable to cover operating expenses. In the following decades one or two paddle steamers tried their hand at trawling but did not persevere and a further attempt to fit engines in an iron-hulled Grimsby smack in 1870 was also a failure. In spite of such setbacks the fishing industry did use steam power in a variety of less direct ways. Steam packets, and later steam trains, had long been used as a means of forwarding fish to inland markets and during the 1860s steam cutters were introduced by Hewitts of Yarmouth to carry cargoes of fish to port from fleets working well out in the North Sea. Other fishing vessels employed steam paddle tugs to tow them to and from grounds when weather conditions were unhelpful to sail.[4] Another innovation rapidly adopted by the fishing industry was the steam capstan; this was a small engine and boiler which took away the back-breaking work of hauling up the trawl by hand. Its introduction in 1876 was preceded by the replacement of rope with steel warps and within a few years the majority of Hull, Grimsby and Scarborough smacks had them fitted.

The first commercially successful steam fishing boats were converted paddle tugs. Legend has it that some sailing smacks dropped their trawls while under tow by these tugs and from this it was just a short step to the tug boat skipper fishing from his own boat. In 1877 a trade depression hit the ports of north east England and the steam tugs were amongst the first casualties. The downturn in trade reduced the tonnage of shipping entering rivers such as the Tyne and meant less towing work for the tugs whose business was already being affected by the growth of steam shipping fleets which required less assistance. As a result, scores of tug boats were laid up and left unemployed at their moorings.

In an attempt to keep his craft earning revenue William Purdy, a North Shields tug master, decided to try his hand as a trawlerman. He fitted out his craft by adapting what gear was available around the port but had to send down to Grimsby for second-hand beam trawl parts. His first trip was in November 1877 and his gamble soon began to pay off. Purdy demonstrated that steam fishing was a commercial proposition and he was aided by the fact that the coal for his fuel bunkers was exceptionally cheap thanks to the trade depression. He was later rewarded with a medal by his grateful North Shields colleagues and there were soon many tug masters with beam trawls.[5] Purdy's lead was swiftly followed not only by other North Shields tugs but also those of Sunderland, Hartlepool and Middlesbrough. However, even before Purdy's venture was underway, a steam fishing craft had been registered for fishing on the Yorkshire coast. In June 1877 a 25 foot steam launch had taken out a fishing registration for operations out of Bridlington Quay.[6] However, this screw driven craft, owned by Kate Wakefield, seems to have been restricted to inshore waters and to have taken fish on a very limited scale. The following year a Whitby steam tug, *Emu*, also took out a fishing registration but, unlike its North Shields counterparts, it specialised in line fishing rather than trawling when towing work was slack.

The converted north eastern paddle tugs did not limit their activities to their home ports but began wandering quite far afield: some tried their luck off the Scottish coast and others became the object of numerous complaints by Yorkshire coast line fishermen during 1878. Before the end of that year their landings became an occasional feature at Scarborough. Soon larger numbers were attracted to grounds off the Yorkshire coast and within two years it was by no means an uncommon sight to see between twelve and twenty north eastern steam trawlers in Scarborough harbour and bay at the same time. The Scarborough fishing industry was somewhat reticent in climbing on to the steam fishing bandwagon, although the port's first steam trawler began operations in the summer of 1878; she was the *Cormorant* and, unlike her Tyneside contemporaries, was not only screw driven but primarily a pleasure yacht. This craft was over 62 feet in length and had been constructed by Messrs Richard Smith of Preston who fitted their own direct acting compound steam engines.[7] She was owned by Henry Hird Foster, a wealthy Scarborough gentleman who took more than a passing interest in the fisheries, and he employed a local yawl skipper, William Appleby, as master. *Cormorant* was fitted with a beam trawl 33½ feet wide and 46 feet long.[8]

The paddle steamers, unlike the trawling smacks, worked only on grounds close to the shore. This was less out of choice than necessity. Being designed primarily for towing work in estuaries and harbours they were not built with an eye to great sea-keeping capacity. This shortcoming was most evident on the open sea and they proved particularly susceptible to bad weather which usually obliged them to run for shelter. They were also heavy on coal and, being designed for towing, space was at a premium: what storage space was available had to be shared between the fuel and the catch. Quite often the latter could only be carried in any quantity by reducing fuel capacity. Such constraints reduced their already limited range.[9] Given such shortcomings, the most profitable mode of operation was for the paddle steamers to leave port for no longer than 24 hours and to fish as continuously as possible. This meant that coal was not wasted in steaming to and from distant grounds and that shelter was never too far away. Thus, their activities were limited to the inshore grounds and in this way they were in direct competition with the inshore fishermen who bitterly resented their incursions. Although they worked different grounds from the smacks, which sought their prey further out, they competed on the same quayside markets. When they chose to concentrate landings on a port such as Scarborough their sheer numbers combined with their catching capacity could flood the market, although, being steam powered, they could usually land their catches before the smacks and thus secure the best prices of the day. Their fish was generally fresher for they returned to port each day, whereas the smacks tended to stay out for several days.

The effect of the rivalry between paddle trawler and smack was particularly apparent at Scarborough where registrations of new sailing craft were reduced to a trickle in the years immediately following Purdy's innovation. Indeed, it was noted towards the end of 1880 that the steamers from the north east 'bid fair to gain a monopoly of the trade'. Their activities left no doubt as to their short-term profitability for at least two of them managed to earn in excess of £70 from just twenty hours fishing.[10] For local fishermen it must have proved galling to see so much profit going to outsiders. As a result, Scarborough fishing interests became involved in steam fishing: a group of five individuals, including Henry Wyrill, banded together to acquire the port's first paddle trawler in December 1880.[11] Called *Dandy*, she was 106 feet long and had been built on the Tyne at Willington Quay back in 1863, and her seventeen years of active service had included duty as a tug at several ports including Dublin and Liverpool. The *Dandy*'s first fishing trip was far from successful for a crew member, James Field, was killed when a chain snapped as the trawl was hauled up and on her return to harbour she hit the pier and damaged one of her paddle boxes.[12] Yet such setbacks did little to quell the growing enthusiasm for these vessels and within a short time a further three vessels, the *Tuskar, Spurn*, and *Star O Tay*, had been purchased and fitted out as trawlers. By the end of 1881 ten such craft had been registered at Scarborough.

The paddle tugs were expensive to purchase; even a well used second-hand craft could rarely be secured for less than £2000 and as their trawling potential became more evident their asking price rose to nearer £3000.[13] This made them about twice as expensive as a brand new trawling smack of the latest design. Such capital was hard to raise and even stretched the resources of the well-established smackowners and fish merchants. Though a few were purchased outright by single individuals, most were acquired by newly formed private, and later limited liability, companies. Amongst the earliest of the latter was the Yorkshire Steam Trawling Company Limited which was founded late in 1881 and within a few months had several vessels in operation.[14] These enterprises had little trouble attracting backers for within a short time £25 shares in one of them, the Star O Tay Steam Trawling and Fishing Company, were changing hands at a premium of 30s.[15] Scarborough, a fashionable resort, attracted the wealthy, many of whom owned houses in the town, and the smackowners were able to persuade many of them to become shareholders.

These pioneering vessels proved prosperous during 1881. Favourable prices, good catches and only limited spells of bad weather meant that they were able to earn an adequate return. Such apparent success seems to have fostered a somewhat over-optimistic view of their potential, leading to what can only be

Scarborough Harbour Late Nineteenth Century
(reproduced by courtesy of Hull Museums and Art Galleries)

described as a mini paddle steamer mania during 1882. In the three months from the beginning of December 1881 to the end of February 1882 a further ten steam-powered fishing vessels were registered and the fleet had soon more than trebled in size.

It was perhaps inevitable that during such a period of buoyant confidence several less than sound ventures were embarked upon. None fitted this description more fully than the Knight of the Cross Steam Trawling Company which raised an initial capital of just over £2931 to purchase a steam tug of the same name. On arrival from Liverpool she proved to be the largest and most powerful member of the Scarborough fleet and her 121 foot long hull contained a vertical side lever steam engine rated at 70 horse-power, which must have given her a voracious appetite for coal.[16] In addition to fishing, this craft, like several of the others, was expected to supplement her income by running passenger trips along the coast in the summer. It was believed that she would be able to fish on grounds much further afield than her contemporaries and trips to the Norwegian coast were mooted. Cargo space was extended as far as possible and, with a full catch on board, the company estimated that the *Knight of the Cross* would be capable of earning £300 from one trip on a good market.[17] Reality proved otherwise. The twenty-year-old paddler was in far from sound condition when purchased and over the next twelve months she was constantly losing valuable fishing time due to costly engineering problems. Furthermore, her entire fishing career, including time laid up for repairs, realised a total income from fish sales of only £477, or an average less than £10 per week. This modest return was far from sufficient to meet outgoings: apart from the costs of repair, the wages and shares due to the crew and sundry other outgoings, the coal bill alone amounted to more than £210. By the end of January 1883 the prospects of profit seemed so bleak that the shareholders decided to cut their losses and wind up the company. Although the craft had cost over £2550 barely a year before, only £800 was obtained from her sale.[18] After all assets were sold off and debts settled, the holder of each share received back less than £2 9s. Since over £48 had been laid out on each share, the entire venture was a disaster. Unfortunately for the Scarborough fishing community, the fate of the Knight of the Cross Steam Trawling Company was merely a precursor of things to come.

The rate at which steam tugs continued to arrive at Scarborough tended to obscure developments in the purpose-built sector. Even before the end of 1880, John Edmond, the principal Scarborough boatbuilder, began to modify a conventional sailing smack he had on the stocks to take a steam engine. This vessel was being built for George Sydney Smith but the engines were quite diminutive, being rated at only ten horse-power and *Young Squire*, as the craft was named, was probably no more than an auxiliary powered sailing smack.[19] The next steam screw vessel to be constructed was a far more radical departure and perhaps can lay claim to being the first purpose-built steam trawler: the *Pioneer* was first registered at Scarborough in October 1881. She was an iron hulled craft, 94 feet in length, thus far larger than any conventional sailing smack. *Pioneer* was built in the yard of John Shuttleworth of Hull and fitted with engines supplied by Messrs Pattison and Atkinson of Newcastle upon Tyne.[20] Though nine individuals held shares in her, the prime mover and principal owner was James Sellers. As on so many occasions over the previous thirty-six years, Sellers was once more to the forefront of new developments at the port. Although he later invested in at least one paddle tug it seems that he held reservations about their long-term viability and saw the future of white fishing in the development of sea-going steam screw trawlers. In February 1882 John Edmond launched his second ketch-rigged steam trawler, the *Kingfisher*: she was wooden but, at 76 feet, much larger than the *Young Squire* and possessed more powerful compound engines rated at 25 horse-power.[21] She was, however, the last of her line, for the construction of large fishing vessels was soon to cease at Scarborough.

During 1883 a further six steam fishing vessels were registered at Scarborough and all but one were screw driven. All were designed to exploit distant water grounds, formerly the preserve of the sailing smacks. An emphasis on iron hulls seems to have ruled out the yard of John Edmond and his like who worked in wood alone. The one paddler to arrive that year was the *Clyde*, worthy of mention since she was newly built and was the first example of her type to begin her seagoing career as a Scarborough fishing vessel.

In spite of the spate of construction, 1883 proved a most unsatisfactory year. Steam paddlers could only remain profitable if worked intensively, yet for much of the year adverse weather conditions prevailed and both paddle tugs and screw steamers were regularly confined to port, the former often for considerable periods. This reduced their earnings considerably. A further problem was directly linked to the limitations of the paddle steamers: because of their great manoeuvrability they could operate on small pockets of ground close to the coast where the smacks did not dare to work for fear of running on to the rocks. By the close of 1883 these grounds had been trawled continuously by paddle steamers for six years with an ever increasing intensity, and, not unnaturally, they began to exhibit marked signs of exhaustion. This lowered catches and earnings for both the paddle steamers and the inshore men with dire results for the industry as a whole.[22] Such disregard for the resource base of the industry, allied to the problems of the weather, produced a harvest of commercial casualties. By February 1884 the Yorkshire Steam Trawling Company, formed some two years earlier, was deeply in debt to the bank and at an extraordinary general meeting the decision was taken to wind it up.[23] Once again, after all assets were sold off and debts paid, the shareholders were left with hardly any return on their investments. Within a short while several other ventures were terminated in a similar fashion and included amongst them was the Star O Tay Steam Trawling Company.

The economic problems afflicting the industry were by no means limited to the steam fleet; all types of fishing experienced downturns in fortune during the mid 1880s. This meant that even those who spread their interests across all sectors were unable to recoup their losses elsewhere. So in the wake of the company failures there followed a number of individual bankruptcies. In March 1885 the vessel owner and fish merchant Edward Rawlinson went under; three months later there was an even heavier crash when the business of Henry Wyrill, for years one of Scarborough's leading entrepreneurs, collapsed with debts totalling more than £12,000. Henry Lamble Woodger, perhaps the main proponent of steam trawling there, also went bankrupt owing more than £4767 in November 1887. This last event followed by only a few months the death of the other leading entrepreneur, James Sellers, in May 1887.

These crises cracked the very foundations of the Scarborough fishing industry and the removal of four such prominent individuals in less than two years particularly weakened the trawling sector, and the fleet declined in strength from the beginning of 1884. By the end of 1887 only sixteen steam trawlers remained compared with twenty-seven at the fleet's peak and from January 1884 to March 1888 not one new steamer was brought to the port.[24] The rot was then halted and several more steamers were registered before the end of the decade, although the *Dolphin* was lost within a few months of construction. Two other craft added at this time, the *Otter* and *Dalhousie*, were to work out of Scarborough until sunk by U boats in 1915. Throughout the 1890s and into the twentieth century the port of Scarborough retained a small steam fleet but it never regained the vitality exhibited in its heyday. In contrast, the steam fleets of Hull, Grimsby, Shields and Aberdeen, went from strength to strength.

To a large degree the lack of development at Scarborough may have been due to its shortcomings in dealing with such vessels. Unlike the Tyne or Humber ports, Scarborough was situated almost as far away from the coalfields as was possible for a north eastern town. Fuel transportation costs were thus that much higher. In addition, the port lacked local marine engineering facilities on a scale to compare with Hull or Shields. A steam vessel which required a heavy overhaul of its engines or boiler had to be dispatched to another port which might involve a costly tow and meant that mechanical failure could not be dealt with as quickly as at some other places. Finally, there was the question of port facilities. Steam trawlers were, in general, about 30 feet longer than smacks and although the harbour at Scarborough had been subject to a major programme of reconstruction, involving the widening and lengthening of the west pier for the fish trade between 1879 and 1882, it could not accommodate a large fleet of steam trawlers. Hull and Grimsby meanwhile had extensive dock and quayside facilities that were better suited and more able to cope with such craft. Similarly, there were numerous places along the Tyne for mooring trawlers once they had discharged their catches at North Shields Fish Quay. Nevertheless, the story of steam trawling on the Yorkshire coast at that time was essentially the story of Scarborough: only two steam fishing craft were registered elsewhere. Although both Bridlington Quay and Whitby possessed harbours that were suitable for such craft, neither had a reputation for operating first class steam fishing vessels of their own, although Whitby sometimes acted as a base for visiting paddle trawlers. Other fishing communities, including Staithes

80

and Filey, lacked even such basic facilities as were available at Scarborough and the success or failure of steam trawling was reliant, so far as the Yorkshire coast was concerned, on just one port.

Throughout the 1890s the Scarborough steam fleet fluctuated in size but generally consisted of about 15 vessels, of which only about six were purpose-built steam screw trawlers. The remainder were converted paddle tugs. Although the shortcomings of these vessels were apparent, the Scarborough owners stuck to them; indeed, a brand new paddle steamer was acquired for fishing as late as 1895.[25] However, because local grounds were so denuded the vessels often had to work inshore grounds off other coasts. In 1897 Scarborough vessels were fishing in the Irish Sea and landing their catches at Milford Haven. Some vessels even tried their luck off the west coast of Ireland. Scarborough was the last fishing port to retain paddle steamers and its final example, *Constance*, remained in service until wrecked at Hartlepool on 22 March 1910.

The purpose-built steam screw trawlers of the early 1890s were grossing on average three times the income of the smacks and their efficiency was further improved by the wholesale adoption of the otter trawl in 1895/6. It is sometimes suggested that this gear was named after the Scarborough steam trawler *Otter*. However, though this craft pioneered the otter trawl at Scarborough the gear had acquired its name by the early 1880s. This trawl kept its net open by means of two large boards known as otter boards thus dispensing with the more cumbersome beam and allowing the net mouth to be even wider. Although steam trawlers found the gear more efficient, it proved unsuitable for use on the less manoeuvrable sailing smacks and hastened their demise. Scarborough's small fleet of steam screw trawlers ranged right across the northern latitudes of the North Sea, but vessels from Hull and Grimsby were beginning to open up grounds off the Icelandic coast. Scarborough men participated in this venture to only a small degree; in 1895 only one of its trawlers was working the northern waters.[26] The port's small deepwater fleet received a boost in September 1900 with the formation of the Scarborough, Hartlepool and North Sea Fishing Company which brought new vessels to the harbour. Even so, its importance as a trawling station continued to shrink over the first decade of the twentieth century as the remaining paddle trawlers were withdrawn from service.

In the last two or three years before the outbreak of the Great War there was some revival in steam fishing and a number of first class vessels was acquired, not only for Scarborough but also for crews from Whitby and Filey. Not all trawled, as some were steam drifters, but the majority were second-hand and acquired by working fishermen in conjunction with local land-based individuals who had capital to spare and an inclination to share in such ventures. But for the outbreak of the Great War there may well have been a wholesale re-expansion of the Yorkshire coast first class fishing fleet.

VIII

The Decline of the Sailing Fleets 1880-1914

The late 1870s saw the zenith of local participation in the herring fishery. Upwards of a hundred yawls and converter smacks, together with large numbers of inshore boats, fitted out each year for a season that might last from July to September. The catching effort thus mobilised was probably about a third of that which the East Anglian ports could muster but it still made the Yorkshire coast herring fleet the second largest in England. Its nearest rival for the position was the Cornish fleet based upon St Ives and Penzance but that was probably only half as strong. Furthermore, most Yorkshire boats carried more gear than Scottish craft; the typical yawl might shoot around 120 nets[1] while the largest boats from north of the border could only carry about eighty.[2] In addition, craft from all over the country congregated at Scarborough and Whitby during the busiest months.

The herring season created a temporary demand for labour that Yorkshire coast towns and villages could not entirely satisfy. Shore-based activities required the import of rullymen, gutters and packers, many of whom travelled up from East Anglia, and on the catching side extra crew members were needed. The number of casuals required had increased because of the growth in drifting rather than lining during the off season; the crew of a great lining vessel had usually been seven and for drifting this was increased to nine. However, the converter smacks carried only five men when trawling so another four crew members had to be recruited for the herring season. Staithes, which stuck to lining, found the extra recruits from amongst its own community but Scarborough had to look to migratory labour, attracted to the port by the prospect of

83

casual work. While regular crewmen were paid by the share, the casuals were paid by the week. Lacking ties with the local community they often contained an unruly element and their employment was looked upon by local owners as a regrettable but necessary evil. Complaints were voiced about their preference for the public house to the sea and their propensity to break contracts by unexpectedly refusing to sail.[3] Yet in the absence of more suitable labour they were crucial to operations during the herring fishery.

The seasons 1880 to 1883 saw a continued increase in activity by visiting vessels and September 1882 saw record landings at both Scarborough and Whitby. However, the Yorkshire coast fleet was experiencing great difficulty in coping with the growing competition and could not maintain its earlier prosperity, which led to a great reduction in the construction of new craft. Scarborough's enthusiasm lay with steam trawlers, which indicates that the herring fishery was less attractive to locals. At Scarborough the number of landings by visiting craft more than trebled between 1879 and 1882 in spite of the inconvenience occasioned by reconstruction of the harbour and at Whitby, where landings had long been dominated by outsiders, a similar trend is discernible.[4]

North of the border, the Scottish herring fisheries had experienced over thirty years of almost continuous growth based on the export of pickle cured herring to eastern European markets. Then suddenly in 1884 this prosperity collapsed through overproduction. Prices fell, curers went bankrupt and the trade did not recover its vitality until the following decade.[5] This collapse of overseas markets had only a limited direct effect upon the Yorkshire coast industry for only a small proportion of its catch went abroad; most of its herring was sold on the home market and little was pickle cured at that time. Nevertheless, the catching sector did suffer as a result of the Scottish troubles. Yorkshire fishermen had little success when pursuing herring in 1883 and hoped to recoup their losses in 1884, but that season was marked by heavy catches which glutted the market and brought prices down to rock bottom. The situation was exacerbated during the first month or so by increased sales of Scottish and Northumbrian herring on the home market. The season, in short, proved unrewarding once more. In 1885 herring landings were again so great that Scarborough fish market was glutted almost daily during the peak season. Quite often the landing price remained as low as 6*d*. a hundred whereas 2*s.* would have been considered unsatisfactory in earlier years.[6] The 1886 season followed a markedly similar pattern and proved particularly poor for the Flamborough fleet of small undecked herring craft. They returned home after a season working out of Scarborough harbour to report that many crews had not even covered their working expenses 'thanks to the prevalence of low prices'.[7]

Within a few years there was an almost complete cessation of herring fishing by the Flamborough men because it had become so unprofitable.[8] The decline in the number of first class Scarborough vessels fitting out for the herring fishery was equally rapid; in 1882 about thirty-two craft went drifting but by 1887 only three made the necessary preparations. By the following year the only fitting out of a local yawl was undertaken by strangers. Early in the following decade no Scarborough first class vessels joined in the herring fishery, which had once provided the most profitable return from the annual round of activity.[9] Paradoxically, the demise of the Yorkshire coast herring fleet gained momentum at precisely the same time as more boats from other areas were being attracted to Scarborough by that very fishery. Throughout the 1880s the number of strangers arriving each season increased almost continually and the size of landings grew. It was this growing outside interest which proved the undoing of the Yorkshire fleet.

In Scotland, after the calamities of 1884, there was a gradual abandonment of the 'engagement system' in which the contract made between fishermen and curers gave the former a guaranteed price for a proportion of their catch but tied them to the port from which the latter operated. The phasing out of this system gave the fishermen greater freedom of movement, if not financial security, and in future it was natural for them to seek out the ports which might prove the most remunerative. There had been an increase in Scottish boats journeying south in the years immediately before 1884, and there were frequent complaints about their methods of working. After 1884 they fished out of English ports in ever-growing numbers, even when their home season was at its peak. Although low prices prevailed at Scarborough and elsewhere they were still more attractive to some Scottish fishermen than the

North Landing Flamborough Late Nineteenth Century
(reproduced by courtesy of Hull Museums and Art Galleries)

prospect of supplying their native curing trade, where supply could soon swamp outlets after the onset of problems in the export markets. Once they had started working off the Yorkshire coasts they may well have been induced to stay longer and visit East Anglia by the fact that their off season long lining activities were meeting with increased competition from the new steam trawling centres of Aberdeen and Granton.

The Yorkshire coast fleets found it difficult to respond success-fully to this outside challenge partly because of the nature and design of their craft; they had been built with a dual purpose in mind and caught white fish, either by lining or trawling, during the off season. Furthermore, mindful of the exposed nature of the coast and the harsh weather encountered, they had been con-structed with sea-keeping qualities to the uppermost and could weather all but the very worst conditions. Thus, they were built broad in the beam but that made them slower than vessels of slimmer hull construction. In the decades before 1880 speed was of marginally less importance as the craft had sometimes remained on the grounds for several days and brought in part of their catch slightly salted rather than all totally fresh. The abandonment of the lugger rig in the 1860s had also lowered top speed. The dandy and gaff rigs may have made the yawls more manoeuvrable when trawling and meant that a smaller crew could handle them, but they also increased the time it took them to return from the fishing grounds.[10] In contrast, Scottish craft made few concessions to white fishing and retained the speedier lugger rig as they increased in size; before 1870 they had rarely exceeded 35 feet in length but by the 1880s the largest of them, known as 'Zulus', regularly exceeded 60 feet.[11] These well-built but slimly hulled craft were constructed with speed as an uppermost factor as it was the Scottish practice to return home from the herring grounds each day. The cured fish trade required their herrings to be as fresh as possible if they were to be processed to the standard entitling them to the fishery board's official brand.

When such craft came south in increasing numbers during the 1880s their increased speed enabled them to beat other boats to harbour and obtain the day's best return. Moreover, when prices were really low — as they were during much of the mid and later 1880s — the practice of landing only when holds were full proved most unprofitable. Overday herring which had been salted at sea had always commanded a lower price than those which reached market within hours of being caught but their value slumped to such an extent that they often proved unsaleable. The ability of the Scottish craft to reach market first came not only from their superior speed but from the fishing practices adopted by their crews. The Yorkshire craft, in common with those from Cornwall and East Anglia, cleared their nets as they came on board. The nets were then passed down one hatch and the herrings down another. The fish were counted for they were to be sold by the hundred. The Scottish fishermen used an entirely different system. Their boats had a very large hold in the centre and they fished using fine deep nets with a very light warp. They kept their nets in the water until ready to return, and this type of gear could be left in the sea in conditions that would force the Englishmen to bring theirs back on board; this was considered advantageous, for there were thought to be more herrings around in a blowing sea. Once hauled in, the Scots bundled their nets down the large hold together with fish, warps, buoys and all. They could then set sail for shore while the other craft were still embroiled in the process of separating fish from nets.[12] The need to count fish was dispensed with as the Scots sold their fish by the cran which is a volume and not numerical measure like the last.

The response of the Yorkshiremen to this competition was to modify their boats in an attempt to give them more speed. The yawls had been built with a clinker hull but this could be made smooth to reduce drag. The 'lands' or grooves were filled in with a feather edge plank and over this was fixed a skin of American elm. Thick bends were put on the outside just below the deck and fastened right through to new knees and frames. The whole process was known as doubling. This undoubtedly improved speed but not sufficiently to make them competitive with the Scottish craft. The yawls thus abandoned the herring fishery and by the 1890s concentrated on white fishing, or were being laid up or sold off. Staithes experimented with vessels of the type used in the south west but again they found it difficult to compete effectively with the Scottish craft.

While landings continued to increase at Scarborough as more and more Scottish craft came south, Whitby began to decline as a herring station from the mid 1880s. A principal cause of this decline was the poor condition of the harbour. The likelihood of a

Scottish Herring Lugger on the River Esk, Whitby Harbour, Late Nineteenth Century
(reproduced by courtesy of Hull Museums and Art Galleries)

vessel sustaining damage while moored there was so high that a number of insurance companies which covered craft from the south west refused to allow them to use the harbour except at their own risk.[13] The Whitby harbour commissioners were hamstrung by lack of finance and unable to respond positively and improvements were not made until their powers were assumed by the urban district council in 1906. As activity declined there was less work for Whitby's resident tug, so it was sold off and many of the remaining sailing craft, deprived of towing facilities in adverse weather conditions, sought other ports.

The Continental markets for Scottish pickle-cured herring revived from 1893 and the trade soon entered a new era of prosperity and expansion that lasted until the opening of the Great War. Landings also continued to increase in England and at Scarborough a peak figure of 193,433 cwt was recorded in 1895. Although East Anglian and Cornish boats continued to participate, the Scottish influence predominated. Scottish pickle curers began to follow the fleets down the North Sea and thus maintain production well after their home season had finished. Scarborough was amongst the ports they visited. Partly because of the nature of their work and partly because of their mobile existence, following the different herring seasons around the coast, these curers used labour-intensive production processes and relied on little fixed plant. Each curer usually employed several gangs of women to clean, split and pack the herring between layers of salt in the barrels. As this called for a level of skill lacking at most fishing stations the curers brought their labour force with them. The women were usually recruited in northern Scotland and could often speak only Gaelic. Others were recruited in Northumberland, from such villages as Seahouses and Beadnell. Additionally, the curer would employ a cooper who would travel ahead of operations to lay in an adequate supply of barrels.

Scarborough's zenith as a herring fishing station was effectively reached before the turn of the century and the harbour was so crowded with craft that large numbers of drifters were forced to unload in the bay. With Whitby out of favour, an attempt was made by the Scottish trade to establish Bridlington Quay as a major herring fishing station in 1899. This worked quite well over that season and the curers returned in 1900. That year they left the port a month earlier than anticipated and did not return the following season. However, the harbour remained a base for the local inshore herring fishers.[14]

The 1900s were marked by the rise of the steam drifter, many of which operated out of Scarborough and by 1905 they were the most important source of herring landings at the port. Over the years up to the Great War this branch of the trade remained prosperous, but although the inshore craft from Staithes, Flamborough and other local stations returned to the fishery, it continued to be dominated by fishermen, merchants and curers from elsewhere.

These years not only witnessed an overall decline of local involvement in the herring fishery, they also saw the demise of white fishing by the first class sailing fleet (Fig. 4). The first real change of note was the transfer of a number of yawls from Filey to Bridlington Quay, some moved about 1875 but most transferred between 1877 and 1881.[15] Filey's lack of harbour facilities was the major reason. Between the 1860s and 1880s several ambitious schemes were floated with the aim of providing a deep water harbour, but all came to naught and by the early twentieth century Filey had lost its fleet of yawls for good.

During the 1870s the Scarborough trawling smacks began to join the boxing fleets sailing out of Hull and Grimsby. These fleets usually remained on the grounds for up to eight weeks and were serviced by fast cutters which took their catches to market. Fleeting enabled the smacks to remain profitable at a time when catches were declining, by allowing each craft to devote more time to fishing, but it was not popular with the fishermen, especially in winter. Transferring the catch from smack to cutter in an open boat was a perilous business and lives were often lost when they were upset in rough seas. Moreover, the fishermen spent eight weeks on a cramped smack with poor provisions and only the most basic of facilities, to say nothing of the absence of normal family life.

Fishing had always been a dangerous pursuit and vessels were regularly wrecked or men lost overboard. In the autumn of 1869 Scarborough lost three vessels with all hands in a ferocious storm which wreaked havoc along the entire seaboard. But the worst disaster occurred after the intensification of fleeting. In March 1883 a sudden storm burst upon the hundreds of vessels fishing on or near the Dogger Bank. Days later, after it had finally blown

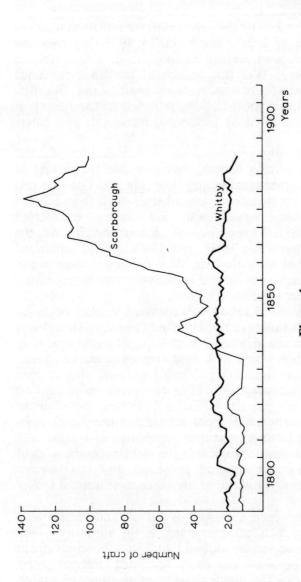

Figure 4.

First Class Fishing Vessels registered in Scarborough and Whitby Customs port areas 1790-1890.

Source: Scarborough and Whitby Custom House Vessel Registers. Details of fleet reconstitution techniques given in R.N.W. Robinson, 'The English Fishing Industry 1790-1914: a case study of the Yorkshire Coast' (Hull University PhD, 1985) Appendix III.

Note: The relationship between the port of registry and the operational or home base for a fishing vessel was much closer in the nineteenth century than is the case in the twentieth.

itself out, it was found that 250 men had perished, forty-three smacks from all ports had sunk, and many more had been damaged.[16]

Scarborough formed its own boxing fleet in the spring of 1880. The moving spirit behind the venture was James Sellers who owned or had an interest in about half of the forty-one vessels which sailed.[17] The port continued to fit out its own fleet for the spring, and sometimes for the summer trawling seasons, for several years. Fleeting did not, however, solve the problems that afflicted the sailing trawlers, it merely eased them for a while. By intensifying the exploitation of the grounds it was possible to increase catches in the short term, but as the underlying problems were caused by stock denudation the longer term problems were made worse and the income earned by trawling smacks over the decade continued to fall. The few craft that proved really successful were the purpose built steam trawlers that came off the stocks in greater numbers as the 1880s wore on. There was still fierce debate about how to revive fortunes, but the long term response was not one of conservation; it was to construct ever more efficient catching vessels and seek out unexploited grounds where stocks had not yet been denuded. This was the principal reason why grounds off Iceland and later off Norway were to become more important than the North Sea in the following decades.

Not surprisingly, Scarborough's fleet of smacks began to shrink. Wrecked craft were not replaced and many others were sold off. Some went to other fishing ports and later became coasters or were purchased by overseas interests, especially the Scandinavians. Even so, a considerable number continued to work throughout the decade. As smacks became progressively less profitable their owners attempted to restore their financial position by cutting costs, which brought about the port's only major industrial confrontation of the nineteenth century. The extension of fleeting had proved unpopular with Hull and Grimsby crews and provoked bitter strikes. The Scarborough owners do not appear to have met such stiff initial opposition for there is little evidence of any organised resistance by their fishermen in the late 1870s and early 1880s. Yet by the mid 1880s vessels were proving so expensive to purchase that few working fishermen had any capital interest in the fleet. Many relied solely on their income from the shares and wages earned through their labour and skill. By 1886 the owners decided that these must be cut if the fleet was to remain viable.

During December 1886 a meeting of Scarborough smackowners decided to alter the terms of the crew engagements. Part of the old terms had stipulated that the owner should receive five per cent of the gross profit for providing the steam capstan, from which he was expected to provide the necessities that kept it operational; under the new arrangements the owner was to receive six and a quarter per cent and the crew were to pay for the fuel. This decision was put to each individual crew as their craft returned to port. The smacks, by virtue of their winter operations, did not arrive in harbour together and their crews, lacking any organisation of their own, reluctantly accepted the new arrangements for a while. Any wish to counter-attack was resisted until the majority of crews were ashore together and the general mass feeling could be gauged. The first such occasion did not occur until most of the boats came in to take advantage of the Easter weekend market by landing on Maunday Thursday, which fell on 14 April 1887. A well-attended meeting was held at the Sandside Coffee House and after protracted discussion the men decided to provide the fuel for the capstans but objected to the deduction of the six and a quarter per cent. On Easter Saturday they refused to return to sea on the owners' terms: in effect some 300 men were on strike. On Easter Sunday the men held a parade through the town followed by attendance at the service at St Thomas's Church.

The strike lasted over a week with no breaking of ranks, but rumours began to circulate that the owners planned to import Grimsby men to work the smacks. The leaders, who included one M. Watkins, swiftly communicated with the Grimsby Fishermen's Protection Society to prevent such a step being taken and to remind them that when the boats of their port had been strike bound Scarborough crews had refused to man them. A reply was soon received pledging support, together with a copy of the Grimsby association's rules, and the suggestion that they form their own union, but by that time the strike had been settled. On the Wednesday following Easter, the owners met in the Sandside Coffee House and offered to return to the original five per cent if the stocker bait was thrown in with the rest of the catch. Stocker bait consisted of fish such as gurnards, rays, monks and dabs which the men had traditionally split amongst themselves: this might yield to the crew between one and nine shillings apiece. This offer was quickly rejected and the owners made a few further concessions. A few days later the strike was settled. The capstan percentage returned to five per cent while the men provided the fuel. Henceforward, the stocker bait was to be divided into six shares of which two were to go to the owner and the others to the men. The three leading crew members, already paid by share on the rest of the catch, were to receive one share each with the remaining one being divided between the two wage men.[18]

Concessions had been made on both sides but, given the adverse economic conditions then prevalent in the industry and the difficulties they faced in organising themselves, the men's achievement was by no means insubstantial. However, there is no evidence that a permanent trade union was then formed by the fishermen. Moreover, the agreement could do little to solve the underlying economic problems which were caused by declining catches on the overworked traditional North Sea grounds. Many owners continued to sell off their vessels and in some cases they had no choice for the series of mid-1880s bankruptcies forced the disposal of craft. Yet in spite of this run down of the fleet there was little obvious unemployment amongst fishermen. In some cases men returned to open boat fishing and earned a smaller income taking crabs and the like. Many others migrated to ports such as Aberdeen, Grimsby, Milford Haven and Fleetwood where steam trawling was thriving. Aberdeen was particularly popular and by 1900 at least one of its trawlers was manned entirely by Scarborough men.[19] In fact, the fishermen seem to have deserted the smacks at a faster rate than the fleet shrank, for by 1890 it was often difficult to find crews, and skippers and first hands being in particularly short supply.[20]

The final nail in the coffin of the Yorkshire coast sailing smack was the introduction of the otter trawl to commercial steam fishing operations in July 1895. This gear was 30 per cent more efficient as a catcher than the beam trawl, although it was difficult to adapt for sailing vessels. The remaining smacks were sold off within a few years; one of them, the *Contrast*, even found its way to Dakar in French West Africa.[21] The more elderly or unseaworthy had a less glamorous fate, being used as either storage hulks or being broken up. By 1900 trawling with first class sailing craft was all but dead at Scarborough.

The story of the great lining activities by yawls over these years is also very much one of an unremitting decline. When they abandoned the pursuit of herrings from the mid 1880s they were usually laid up each summer and used for lining over the remainder of the year. Partly because of their reduced activities, and partly because of the impoverished nature of the grounds they traditionally worked, their yearly income slumped dramatically. In their heyday during the 1850s and 1860s many yawls grossed in excess of £900 annually but by 1892 few of them were managing to earn more than £200 over a year.[22] In spite of their greater obsolescence a number of the Yorkshire yawls outlasted the Scarborough sailing smacks by several years. The *Tranquility* and *Prosperous*, built in 1866 and 1858 respectively, were still working when the second decade of the twentieth century opened. Both had long since repaid their original outlay many times over and factors such as depreciation were far behind them. As their resale value was practically nil some fishermen found it worthwhile to continue to work them for a few months each year, spending the absolute minimum on maintenance.

Whitby did not possess such a fleet of yawls, although some locals had acquired smacks during the 1880s. Most of the vessels still registered at the port's Custom House by the late 1890s worked out of Staithes and the last two were laid up after 1909. During the final years their annual pattern of usage was somewhat different from that of Scarborough and Bridlington yawls, for they were employed only during the summer months and spent the rest of the year laid up in Whitby harbour.

The Great War terminated the careers of the last Yorkshire yawls. Fishing in the North Sea during the conflict was both restricted and hazardous and limited to steam trawlers and small inshore craft. Shortages of raw materials made their wood and copper fittings valuable and all were broken up, except the *William Clowes*. That yawl acted as headquarters of the Scarborough Yacht Club until it too was broken up in 1921.[23]

This catalogue of decline was added to by the inshore fisheries. Indeed, those working inshore waters probably endured the greatest hardship. By the 1870s they were suffering from an acute bait shortage which did not ease greatly in the following decades. Furthermore, as the herring fishery was given over by many because of poor financial returns in the later 1880s, more effort was put into taking crabs and lobsters, which in turn led to renewed reports of falling yields. However, it was probably the long line fishery that was most affected by falling yields during the 1880s. From the later 1870s certain inshore grounds were subject to the full blast of exploitation by the paddle trawlers, and continuous steam trawling caused a spate of complaints about damage to stocks. In a report published by the 1885 Royal Commission on Trawling, Professor McIntosh of St Andrews University found that half of the fish that paddle steamers trawled up were immature and not large enough to be marketed.[24] The inshore men felt the effects more acutely than the paddle trawlers for at least the latter could try distant stretches of coast when catches fell off. In 1890 the newly-formed North Eastern District Sea Fisheries Committee passed a bye-law banning most inshore trawling but by then much damage had been done. The numbers employed in the inshore fisheries at Whitby fell away. Yet, unlike the men of Scarborough, they seemed loathe to move to the rising ports of Aberdeen and Fleetwood probably because of the dislike of trawling. Many Staithes fishermen who left the trade are reported to have gone into the iron yards of Middlesbrough.[25] Further down the coast, at Bridlington and Flamborough, others supplemented their income by catering for the tourist trade during the summer months and this became of particular importance in the twentieth century.

The North Eastern District Sea Fisheries Committee also introduced new conservation measures for the shell fisheries including close seasons for crabbing and although these met with almost universal approval at first, a clamour arose for their removal as fishermen became more and more dependent on crabbing for their livelihood. An enquiry into the matter was held in 1905 and the close season for crabs was then abolished,[26] thus setting back the conservationist cause.

One result of the continuing bait shortage was a gradual shift in attitude in the early twentieth century towards trawling by many of the smaller communities. In the early 1890s most inshore stations still reviled the practice with the exception of Bridlington Quay, whose fishermen were sometimes on hostile terms with the Flamborough men because of this. Yet little more than a decade later many were to take up the practice and call for its prohibition, inside large stretches of the three mile limit, to be lifted. Only

Table 3

Numbers Occupied as Fishermen

	East Riding§	North Riding	Total
1830	n.a.	n.a.	522
1840	n.a.	n.a.	862
1845	n.a.	n.a.	946
1851	222	704	926
1861	307	756	1063
1871	323	1029	1352
1881*	417	1215	1632
1891	386	1050	1436
1901	400	678	1078
1911	582	599	1181

§ excluding Hull

n.a. not available

*   At the 1881 Census fishermen arriving in port during the 14 days following the Censal data were included. While this may have affected the East and North Riding totals to some extent, its influence was insufficient to alter the general trend as shown by the size of the fishing fleets.

Sources: Herring Fishery Commissioners' Records: 1830, 1840 and 1845; Census Returns: 1851-1911.

Flamborough remained resolutely opposed and even its fishermen were to adopt the practice during the Great War when the bye-law in question was suspended in the face of food shortages.

Shortage of capital was a continuing problem for the inshore fisheries, especially after 1900. By 1910 it was evident that a small vessel could be made more profitable if adapted to motor power but lack of finance meant that few Yorkshire coast inshore boats were fitted with oil engines before 1914. During the War, however, the artificial boom conditions created by the food shortages enabled many fishermen to motorise their craft and the process of conversion from sail continued afterwards.

By the early twentieth century all sectors of the Yorkshire coast fishing industry were declining. The labour force reached its zenith in 1881 when a total of 1632 fishermen were enumerated; by 1911 there were 1181 and a number of these were part-timers (Table 3). Stations such as Staithes and Filey, which had once sustained sizeable first class fishing fleets in their own right, had been reduced to the status of inshore bases and the resurgence of Bridlington Quay, Scarborough and Whitby as off-shore fishing centres was still decades away. In part, such decline was to be expected as the trawling sector of the trade became increasingly sophisticated, based on ports with considerable harbour facilities and marine engineering back up. Yet, in part, decline was also a consequence of the pace of the earlier expansion and the lack of adequate conservationist measures which led to a denudation of many North Sea white fishing grounds and a rush to open up new deep water grounds in the far north. The resultant reliance upon such grounds off the coasts of other nations was to be at the root of many problems afflicting the British fishing industry during the second half of the twentieth century.

Notes

Notes for pages 1-10

I   The Economic and Social Background

1. R.G. Couzen, 'The Growth and Character of Whitby', in *A Survey of Whitby*, ed. G.H.J. Dough (Windsor, 1958) p. 51.
2. L. Charlton, *A History of Whitby* (York, 1779) p. 338.
3. *Hull Advertiser*, 9 Nov. 1827.
4. J. Dykes, *Smuggling on the Yorkshire Coast* (Clapham, 1978) pp. 7 and 30.
5. G.A. North, *Teesside's Economic Heritage* (Cleveland, 1975) p. 25.
6. R.Schofield, *The Scarborough Guide* (Hull, 1796) p. 106.
7. B. Waites, 'The Medieval Ports and Trade of North East Yorkshire', *Mariner's Mirror,* 63 (1977) pp. 144-6.
8. D.S. Walker, *Whitby Fishing* (Whitby, 1968) n.p.
9. Kingston upon Hull Record Office (hereafter KHRO), BRW/5/12, 31 Oct. 1653.
10. Ibid., 31 Oct. 1653.
11. P. Heath, 'North Sea Fishing in the Fifteenth Century', *Northern History*, 3 (1968) p. 58-61.
12. Walker, n.p.
13. J.W. Ord, *The History and Antiquities of Cleveland* (1846) p. 357.
14. R. Fisher, *Flamborough Village and Headland* (Hull, 1894) p. 143.
15. Ibid.
16. *Scarborough Gazette*, 24 Sept. 1884.

II   The Later Eighteenth-Century Fishing Industry

1. G. Young, *A History of Whitby and the Vicinity*, vol. 2 (Whitby, 1817) pp. 820-3.
2. Hull Custom House, Bridlington Register of Boat Licenses, 1813-16.
3. A first class vessel was defined thus by the Customs Commissioners. According to the Act of 1786, which introduced compulsory registration of all merchant craft, it was a decked boat or ship of more than 15 tons burthen. On the Yorkshire coast such a definition is useful for it divides the inshore or open boats from the larger decked vessels that fished the deeper water grounds.
4. Young, pp. 820-3.

Notes for pages 10-23

5. E.W. Bedell, *An Account of Hornsea* (Hull, 1848) p. 97.
6. House of Commons Journal, vol. 72, 4 July 1817.
7. Board of Trade Report on Relations between Owners, Masters and Men, *A. and P.*, 1882 XVII, *Minutes of Evidence*, Qs 2556-7.
8. Charlton, pp. 362-3.
9. Young, pp. 820-3.
10. J. Cole, *The History and Antiquities of Filey in the County of York* (Scarborough, 1819) pp. 93-5.
11. Young, pp. 820-3.
12. 'Captain Washington's Report on Fishing Vessels', *A. and P.* 1849 LI p. 277.
13. Cole, pp. 93-5.
14. Young, pp. 820-3.
15. Ibid.
16. R.C. on Sea Fisheries, 1866 XVII-XVIII *Minutes of Evidence,* Qs 5050-52.
17. Register House, Edinburgh (hereafter RHE) AF1/6, 4 March 1823.
18. *Whitby Gazette*, 9 June 1860.

III Markets, Products and War, 1780s to the 1810s

1. Charlton, pp. 362-3.
2. E. Baines, *History, Directory and Gazetteer of the County of York* (Leeds, 1822) p. 587.
3. W.H. Chaloner, 'Trends in Fish Consumption', in *Our Changing Fare,* eds T.C. Barker, J.C. McKenzie and J. Yudkin (1966) p. 108.
4. KHRO, BRW/5/12, 31 Oct. 1653, BRW/5/15, 17 Jan. 1680.
5. R.C. on Sea Fisheries, 1866 XVII-XVIII, *Minutes of Evidence*, Qs 5610-20.
6. R.C. on Irish Fisheries, 1836 XXXII, *Appendix,* p. 149.
7. Cole, pp. 94-6.
8. R.Schofield, *The Scarborough Guide* (Hull, 1796) pp. 110-11.
9. Scarborough Public Library, Scarborough Harbour Commissioners' Minutes (hereafter SPL, SHCM), Account of All Monies collected, 1835-1843'.
10. *Hull Advertiser*, 5 Aug. 1796 and 15 Oct. 1802.
11. T. Hinderwell, *The History and Antiquities of Scarborough* (Scarborough, 1832) pp. 207-8.
12. D. Defoe, *A Tour through the Whole Island of Great Britain* (1726; Penguin ed. 1971) p. 532.
13. A.R. Michell, 'The European Fisheries in Early Modern Europe'

Notes for pages 23-33

in *The Cambridge Economic History of Europe* eds E.E. Rich and C.H. Wilson, vol. 5 (1977) pp. 141-2.
14. Papers relating to Salt Duties, *A. and P.*, 1817 XIV, 383.
15. R. Perren, *The Meat Trade in Britain 1840-1914* (1978) p. 217.
16. S.C. on British Herring Fisheries 1800, 1803 X, *Report* p. II.
17. G.S. Clarke, 'The Location and Development of the Hull Fishing Industry' (Hull University MSc, 1957) pp. 21-2.
18. PRO, CUST., 90/7.
19. Ibid., CUST., 90/7.
20. A. Smith, *An Inquiry into the Nature and Causes of the Wealth of Nations* (1776; Routledge ed. 1946) pp. 345-8.
21. For example: PRO, ADM7/381 and ADM7/385; also KHRO, Schedule 56/1386/132.
22. B. Farnhill, *Robin Hood's Bay* (Clapham, 1966) pp. 46-7.
23. PRO, Whitby Register of Boat Licenses, 1813-16.
24. *Hull Advertiser*, 13 Mar. 1801.
25. KHRO, BRW/5/12, 31 Oct. 1653.
26. *Hull Advertiser*, 13 Mar. 1801.
27. *Hull Advertiser*, 3 Jan. 1795.
28. *Leeds Intelligence*, 14 Aug. 1797.
29. North Yorkshire County Record Office (hereafter NYCRO) Scarborough Letters, 23 Mar. 1813, 4 Apr. 1813 and 6 Apr. 1813.

IV   New Developments 1815-1840

1. Scarborough and Whitby Custom House Vessel Registers 1815-19.
2. R.N.W. Robinson, 'The English Fishing Industry 1790-1914: a case study of the Yorkshire Coast' (Hull University PhD, 1985) p. 76.
3. Ibid., p. 71.
4. RHE, AFI/9, 9 Oct. 1832.
5. Ibid., AFI/6, 9 Feb. 1822.
6. Ibid., AFI/6, 4 June 1822.
7. Ibid., AFI/6, 6 Sept. 1825.
8. Robinson, PhD Thesis, 84.
9. House of Commons Journal: vol. 81, 20 Feb. 1826 and 24 Feb. 1826; vol. 83, 17 Mar. 1828; vol. 85, 5 Apr. 1830 and 25 May 1830.
10. C.A. Goodlad, *Shetland Fishing Saga* (Shetland, 1971) pp. 132-5.
11. J.M. Bellamy, *The Trade and Shipping of Nineteenth-Century Hull* (Hull, 1971: repr. 1979) pp. 24-5.
12. *Hull and Eastern Counties Herald*, 15 Dec. 1842 and KHRO., Schedule 56/162/1-2.

Notes for pages 34-49.

13. RHE, AFI/5, 26 Nov. 1819 and 6 Sept. 1825.
14. Ibid., AFI/9, 30 Sept. 1834.
15. *Yorkshire Gazette*, 12 Oct. 1833.
16. *Whitby Repository*, 1833.
17. RHE, AFI/10, 27 Sept. 1836.
18. R. Ainsworth, *Scarborough Guide* (Scarborough, 1844) p. 54.
19. Scarborough Custom House Vessel Register 1833 no. 6.
20. Ibid., 1834 and 1835.
21. 'Captain Washington's Report on Fishing Vessels', *A. and P.* 1849 LI, *Appendix* p. 22.
22. E. March, *Inshore Craft of Great Britain* (1970) pp. 132-3.
23. G. Young, *A Picture of Whitby* (2nd ed., Whitby, 1839) pp. 198-200.
24. RHE, AFI/10, 29 Aug. 1837 and 17 May 1838.
25. Ibid., AFI/11, 28 Apr. 1840.

V Railways and the Rise of Trawling

1. G. Reussner, 'The Whitby to Pickering Railway, Income and Traffic', *Moors Line*, 55 (Spring 1981) pp. 15-17.
2. *Hull and Eastern Counties Herald*, 9 Sept. 1839.
3. Reussner, pp. 15-17.
4. *Hull and Eastern Counties Herald*, 3 Mar. 1842.
5. Ibid., 27 Jan. 1842.
6. *Hansard*, 20 Mar. 1842, p. 1214.
7. Robinson, PhD Thesis, p. 121.
8. PRO, ADM7/384, 11 May 1790.
9. S.C. on British Herring Fisheries, 1800 X, *First Report*, pp. 130-1.
10. R.M. Northway, 'The Devon Fishing Industry 1760-1860' (Exeter University MA, 1970) pp. 81-3.
11. Robinson, PhD Thesis, pp. 136-40.
12. *Yorkshire Gazette*, 30 July 1831.
13. *Hull Rockingham*, 9 June 1832.
14. *Yorkshire Gazette*, 17 Sept. 1833.
15. Scarborough Custom House Vessel Register, 12 Aug. 1839 and 18 Mar. 1840.
16. J. Nicholson, *Food from the Sea* (1979) p. 61.
17. R.C. on Sea Fisheries, 1866 XVII-XVIII, *Report* p. xxi.
18. J.M. Bellamy, 'Pioneers of the Hull Trawl Fishing Industry', *Mariner's Mirror*, 51 (May 1965) pp. 185-6.
19. *Leeds Mercury*, 20 Jan. 1845.

Notes for pages 49-65

20. *The Times*, 20 Jan. 1845.
21. *Hull Advertiser*, 24 Jan. 1845.
22. This account is based on entries in the Scarborough and Whitby Custom House Vessel Registers 1849-59.
23. G.L. Alward, *The Sea Fisheries of Great Britain and Ireland* (Grimsby, 1932) pp. 336-342.
24. Scarborough Custom House Vessel Register, 9 July 1845.
25. Robinson, PhD Thesis, pp. 159-61.
26. R.C. on Sea Fisheries, 1866 XVII-XVIII, *Minutes of Evidence* Q.6676.
27. Scarborough Custom House Vessel Register, 15 Nov. 1867 and 11 Nov. 1868.
28. E. Dade, 'Trawling under Sail on the North East Coast', *Mariner's Mirror*, 18 (1932) pp. 363-5.

VI The Herring, Line, and Inshore Fisheries 1840-1879

1. M. Gray, *The Fishing Industries of Scotland 1790-1914* (Aberdeen, 1979) p. 59.
2. RHE, AFI/13, 10 May 1842.
3. *Sea Fisheries of England and Wales,* Report of F. Buckland and S. Walpole, *A. and P.* 1879 XVII, *Minutes of Evidence*, p. 109.
4. E. March, *Sailing Drifters* (1952) pp. 58-9.
5. *Whitby Gazette*, 6 Mar. 1858.
6. Ord, pp. 299-300.
7. *Whitby Gazette*, 30 Aug. 1857.
8. R.C. on Trawling, 1885 XVI, *Minutes of Evidence*, Qs 8655-7.
9. *Whitby Gazette,* 9 June 1860.
10. R.C. on Sea Fisheries, 1866 XVII-XVIII, *Minutes of Evidence,* Qs 5990-3.
11. SPL, SHCM, 20 Feb. 1864 and 12 Jan. 1865.
12. *Scarborough Gazette*, 10 and 24 Nov. 1887.
13. *Whitby Gazette*, 30 Sept. 1870.
14. *Scarborough Gazette*, 11 Oct. 1883.
15. RHE, AFI/13, 3 May 1842 and 10 May 1843.
16. RHE, AFI/13, 3 May 1842, 10 May 1843, and 8 May 1844.
17. R.C. on Sea Fisheries, 1863-6, 1866 XVII-XVIII, *Minutes of Evidence*, Qs 5524 and 6443.
18. *Scarborough Gazette*, 23 Feb. 1865.
19. Scarborough Custom House Vessel Register, 22 July 1862.
20. Robinson, PhD Thesis, pp. 202-6.

Notes for pages 66-81.

21. Ibid., pp. 205-6.
22. R.C. on Sea Fisheries, 1866 XVII-XVIII, *Minutes of Evidence* Q. 6737.
23. Robinson, PhD Thesis, pp. 208-10.
24. R.C. on Sea Fisheries, 1866 XVII-XVIII, *Minutes of Evidence,* Q. 6799.
25. Robinson, PhD Thesis, pp. 212-16.

VII   The Establishment of Steam Fishing 1877-1914

1. D. Butcher, *The Driftermen* (Reading, 1979) p. 144.
2. E. Morey, *The North Sea* (1968) p. 130.
3. G.N. Von Tunzelman, *Steam Power and British Industrialisation to 1860* (Oxford, 1978) p. 292.
4. Robinson, PhD Thesis, pp. 300-1.
5. Anon., *The Origin of the Tyne Lifeboat Service and of the Tynemouth Volunteer Life Brigade* (North Shields, 1928) pp. 5-11.
6. Hull Custom House Fishing Vessel Register, 27 June 1877.
7. Scarborough Custom House Vessel Register, 3 Aug. 1878.
8. *Sea Fisheries of England and Wales*, Report of F. Buckland and S. Walpole, *A. and P.* 1879 XVII, *Minutes of Evidence,* p. 105.
9. R.C. on Trawling, 1885 XVI, *Minutes of Evidence*, Qs 8018 and 10, 317.
10. *Whitby Gazette*, 24 Dec. 1880.
11. Scarborough Custom House Vessel Register, 29 Dec. 1880.
12. A. Godfrey, *Yorkshire Fishing Fleets* (Clapham, 1974) p. 24.
13. *Scarborough Gazette*, 19 Jan. 1882.
14. Ibid., 5 Jan. 1882.
15. Ibid., 11 May 1882.
16. Scarborough Custom House Vessel Register, Jan. 1882.
17. *Scarborough Gazette,* 15 Jan. 1882.
18. Scarborough Public Library, Maritime Papers and Letters.
19. Scarborough Custom House Vessel Register, 15 Sept. 1881.
20. Ibid., 19 Oct. 1881.
21. Ibid., 16 Feb. 1882.
22. Robinson, PhD Thesis, pp. 323-8.
23. *Scarborough Gazette*, 28 Feb. 1884.
24. Robinson, PhD thesis, pp. 325-30.
25. Scarborough Custom House Vessel Register, 17 Sept. 1895.
26. SCH, Registrar General of Seamen Letter Book, 24 Apr. 1895.

Notes for pages 83-99.

VIII   The Decline of the Sailing Fleets 1880-1914

1.   R.C. on Sea Fisheries, 1866 XVII-XVIII, *Minutes of Evidence,* Q. 6039.
2.   Gray, p. 83.
3.   Board of Trade Report on Relations between Owners, Masters and Men, 1882 XVII, *Minutes of Evidence, A. and P.,* Qs. 2881 and 2913.
4.   Scarborough and Whitby Harbour Commissioners Ledgers and Minutes.
5.   Gray, pp. 146-7.
6.   *Scarborough Gazette,* 1 Oct. 1885.
7.   Ibid., 21 Oct. 1886.
8.   Fisher, p. 49.
9.   Robinson, PhD Thesis, p. 343.
10.   E. Dade, 'The Old Yorkshire Yawls', *Mariner's Mirror,* 91 (1933) p. 190.
11.   Gray, pp. 83-4.
12.   Dade, 'Yorkshire Yawls', pp. 190-1.
13.   *Whitby Gazette,* 19 Sept. 1885.
14.   HCRO, North Eastern District Sea Fisheries Committee Minutes, 5 Dec. 1900.
15.   Hull Custom House, Register of Fishing Vessels, 18 Nov. 1877 to 5 Jan. 1881.
16.   Godfrey, pp. 16-19.
17.   *Scarborough Gazette,* 6 May 1880.
18.   Robinson, PhD Thesis, pp. 350-4.
19.   *Scarborough Gazette,* 13 Sept. 1900.
20.   SCH, Board of Trade Letter Book, 14 May 1891.
21.   Scarborough Custom House Vessel Register, 22 July 1862.
22.   *Scarborough Post,* 4 Aug. 1893.
23.   Dade, 'Yorkshire Yawls', pp. 183-7.
24.   R.C. on Trawling, 1885 XVI, *Report,* p. xix.
25.   Ibid., *Minutes of Evidence,* Q. 10,004.
26.   HCRO, NEDSFCM, 'Mr Tosh's Report on the Crab and Lobster Fisheries' [typescript], 6 Nov. 1905.

Bibliography

Primary Sources

1. Fishery Board Records. This body administered the British herring fisheries from 1809 and the cod, ling and hake fisheries from 1820. It oversaw many curing operations in England and Wales until 1850 after which its activities were confined to Scotland. Its original title was the Board of British Herring Fisheries. The records are in the Register House, Edinburgh, under the classification AF.
2. North Eastern District Sea Fisheries Committee Records: Humberside County Record Office, Beverley, Yorkshire.
3. Whitby Custom House Vessel Registers and Whitby Harbour Commissioners Minutes: North Yorkshire County Record Office, Northallerton.
4. Scarborough Custom House Vessel Registers: North Yorkshire County Record Office, Northallerton.
   Scarborough Harbour Commissioners' Minutes: Scarborough Public Library.
5. Bridlington Custom House Vessel Registers: Kingston upon Hull City Record Office.
   Documents relating to Bridlington Harbour: Brynmor Jones Library, Hull University.
6. Hull Custom House Vessel Registers: Kingston upon Hull Record Office.
7. British Transport Commission Records: Public Record Office, Kew.

Parliamentary Reports and Papers

S.C. on British Herring Fisheries, 1785 XVII.
S.C. on British Fisheries, 1798 1803 X.
S.C. on British Herring Fisheries 1800 1803 X.
Papers relating to Salt Duties, *A. and P.* 1817 XIV.
R.C. on Irish Fisheries, 1836 XXXII.
Captain Washington's Report on Fishing Vessels; *A. and P.* 1849 LI, *Appendix.*
R.C. on Sea Fisheries, 1866 XVII-XVIII.
Report on Crab and Lobster Fisheries of England, Wales, Scotland and Ireland, *A. and P.* 1877 XXIV.
Sea Fisheries in England and Wales. Report of F. Buckland and S. Walpole, *A. and P.* 1878-9 XVII.
Report of W.H. Higgins Esq., Q.C., on the Outrages Committed by Foreign upon British Fishermen in the North Sea, *A. and P.* 1881 LXXXII.
Board of Trade Report on Relations between Owners, Masters and Men, *A. and P.* 1882 XVII.
R.C. on Trawling, 1885 XVI.
S.C. on Sea Fisheries 1894 XV.
Annual Returns of Trade and Navigation, 1868-1914.
Annual Sea Fisheries Statistical Tables, 1886-1914.

Hansard.
House of Commons Journals.

Theses

Clarke, G.S.   'The Location and Development of the Hull Fishing Industry' (Hull Univ. MSc, 1957).

Northway, A.M.   'The Devon Fishing Industry 1760-1860' (Exeter Univ. MPhil, 1970).

Robinson, R.N.W.   'The English Fishing Industry 1790-1914: a case study of the Yorkshire Coast' (Hull Univ. PhD, 1985).

Newspapers

Hull Advertiser.
Hull and Eastern Counties Herald.
Hull Rockingham.
Leeds Intelligencer.
Leeds Mercury.
Scarborough Gazette.
Scarborough Post.
The Times.
Whitby Gazette.
Whitby Repository.
Yorkshire Gazette.

Secondary Sources
Place of publication is London unless otherwise specified.

Alward, G.L.   *The Sea Fisheries of Great Britain and Ireland* (Grimsby, 1932).

Anon.   *The Origins of the Tyne Lifeboat Service and the Tynemouth Volunteer Life Brigade* (North Shields, 1928).

Ainsworth, R.   *Scarborough Guide* (Scarborough, 1844).

Bagwell, P.S.   *The Railway Clearing House* (1968).

Baines, E.I.   *History, Directory and Gazetteer of the County of York* (Leeds, 1822).

Bedell, E.W.   *An Account of Hornsea* (Hull, 1848).

Bellamy, J.M.   'Pioneers of the Hull Trawl Fishing Industry', *Mariner's Mirror,* vol. 51 (May, 1965).

Bellamy, J.M.   *The Trade and Shipping of Nineteenth Century Hull* (East Yorkshire Local History Series, no. 27: Hull, 1971, repr. 1979).

Buckley, J.   *The Outport of Scarborough 1602-1853* (n.d.).

Butcher, D.   *The Driftermen* (Reading, 1979).

Chaloner, W.H.   'Trends in Fish Consumption', *Our Changing Fare*, eds. T.C. Barker, J.C. MacKenzie and J. Yudkin (1966).

Charlton, L.   *A History of Whitby* (York, 1779).

Cole, J.   *The History and Antiquities of Filey in the County of York* (Scarborough, 1819).

Couzen, R.G.   'The Growth and Character of Whitby' in *A Survey of Whitby* ed. G.H.J. Dough (Windsor, 1958).

Dade, E.   'Trawling under Sail on the North East Coast', *Mariner's Mirror,* vol. 18 (1932).

Dade, E.   'The Old Yorkshire Yawls', *Mariner's Mirror,* vol. 19 (1933).

Dykes, J.   *Smuggling on the Yorkshire Coast* (Clapham, 1978).

Farnhill, B.   *Robin Hood's Bay* (Clapham, 1966).

Fisher, R.   *Flamborough Village and Headland* (Hull, 1894).

Gillett, E.   *A History of Grimsby* (Hull, 1970).

Godfrey, A.   *Yorkshire Fishing Fleets* (Clapham, 1974).

Goodlad, C.A.   *Shetland Fishing Saga* (Shetland, 1972).

Gray, M.   *The Fishing Industries of Scotland 1790-1914* (Aberdeen, 1979).

Heath, P.   'North Sea Fishing in the Fifteenth Century', *Northern History*, vol. 3 (1968).

Hinderwell, T.   *The History and Antiquities of Scarborough* (Scarborough, 1832).

Jackson, G.   *Hull in the Eighteenth Century* (Hull, 1972).

Kendall, C.   *God's Hand in the Storm* (1870).

March, E.   *Sailing Drifters* (1953).

March, E.   *Inshore Craft of Great Britain* (1970).

Morey, G.   *The North Sea* (1968).

Michell, A.R.   'The European Fisheries in Early Modern History', *The Cambridge Economic History of Europe* vol. 4, eds. E.E. Rich and C.H. Wilson (1977).

Nicholson, J.   *Food from the Sea* (1979).

North, G.A.   *Teesside's Economic Heritage* (Cleveland, 1975).

Ord, J.W.   *The History and Antiquities of Cleveland* (1846).

Perren, R.   *The Meat Trade in Britain 1840-1914* (1978).

Reussner, G.   'The Whitby and Pickering Railway: Income and Traffic' in *Moors Line* (Spring, 1981).

Rowntree, A.   *History of Scarborough* (1931).

Schofield, R.   *The Scarborough Guide* (Hull, 1796).

Sharp, Sir C.   *History of Hartlepool* (Durham, 1816).

Shaw, G.   *Our Filey Fishermen* (1867).

Smith, A.   *An Inquiry into the Nature and Causes of the Wealth of Nations* (1776, Routledge ed. 1946).

Thompson, M.   *Historical Sketches of Bridlington* (Bridlington, 1821).

Tunstall, J.   *The Fishermen* (1962).

Von Tunzelman, G.N.   *Steam Power and British Industrialisation to 1860* (Oxford 1978).

Waites, B.   'The Medieval Ports and Trade of North East Yorkshire'

	in *Mariner's Mirror*, vol. 63 (1977).
Walker, D.S.	*Whitby Fishing* (Whitby, 1968).
Young, G.	*A History of Whitby and the Vicinity*, vol. 2 (Whitby, 1817).
Young, G.,	*A Picture of Whitby* (1821, 2nd ed. 1839).